MOTOR CYCLE
A D V E N T U R E S

In The Southern Appalachians

Asheville NC
•
The Blue Ridge Parkway
•
NC High Country

By Hawk Hagebak

THIS SHOULD BE YOU!
~ Hawk

milestone press

almond, nc

Milestone Press, PO Box 158, Almond NC 28702

Book design by Ron Roman/Treehouse Communications
www.treehousecomm.com

Cover and interior photos (except as indicated)
by Mary Ellen Hammond & Jim Parham

Maps by Jim Parham

Library of Congress Cataloging-in-Publication Data

Hagebak, Hawk, 1967-
    Motorcycle adventures in the southern Appalachians: Asheville, NC, the Blue Ridge
Parkway, NC high country / by Hawk Hagebak.
        p. cm.
    ISBN 1-889596-11-6 (alk. paper)
    1. Motorcycling—North Carolina—Guidebooks. 2. North Carolina—Guidebooks.
    I. Title

GV1059.522.N8 H35 2002
917.56'8044—dc21   2001059093

Printed in the United States on recycled paper.

Acknowledgments

Without the assistance of family, friends, and even total strangers, this second book in my series of motorcycle adventures would have been little more than a series of crude maps on coffee-stained napkins.

The people of the Southern Appalachians provided colorful stories that brought to life the regional information I gleaned during my research. Fellow motorcyclists were equally open in their sharing of information and advice. Their opinions and stories from the road, as well as honest critiques about some of my other writings, made a difference in how this book was written and presented.

My beautiful and gracious wife Lisa patiently read over this entire work and knew exactly the word I was looking for when I asked, "What's the word for...?" Our daughters Shannon, Savannah, Stacie, and Annabelle provided me with endless encouragement. My parents provided their own brand of encouragement by asking, "So, are you rich and famous yet?" My brothers Cory, Christen, and Beaumont and sisters Lara and Olivia provided support by believing that I could pull off just about anything I was willing to try.

Finally, many of my nonriding friends listened to me discuss this guide *ad nauseam*. In the face of my attempts to tone down my enthusiasm, they stood fast and supported me, but are as relieved as anyone that they won't have to listen to every detail of my creative process for a while.

It takes many people to produce a book of this nature, and I thank all of them. That done, I think I'll go ride the tread off another pair of tires.

Contents

Introduction 6

Code of the Road 8

Summary of State
Motorcycle Laws 11

Tips for the Road 12

The Asheville Area

THE ASHEVILLE AREA

Exploring Asheville 20

City Escape 28

Lake Lure Run 32

Hot Springs 36

Trust & Luck 42

Climbing Mount Mitchell 46

Buncombe Turnpike 52

Hail Caesar 56

Mount Pisgah Loop 60

THE FAR WEST

Tourist Tour 68

Top of the Parkway 76

Smokin' Dragon 84

Cullasaja Gorge Run 90

Cradle Loop 96

Franklin Loop 100

THE HIGH COUNTRY

Little Switzerland Loop 106

Burnsville Loop 110

Murder Mountain 114

The Far West

Boone & Banner Elk 120

Grandfather Loop 128

Blowing Rock 136

Watauga Loop 140

Fresco Tour 146

Stations Loop 152

The Backbone 156

Mount Rogers Scenic Byway 164

APPENDIX

Places to Stay, Play, Eat,
and Shop 171

The High Country

Introduction

For groups and individuals alike, motorcycling has grown into a huge sport. There are endless choices of bikes and components, and anyone's tastes can be satisfied. One element remains constantly popular with all motorcyclists, and that is the road. Sure, bikes are arguably prettier than ever, but given a chance to ride or stare at a bike, most of us will choose to ride.

ROADS & BIKES: THE EVOLUTION OF A SPORT

Since the invention of the Michaux-Perreaux velocipede motorcycle (known as the "boneshaker") in 1869, bikes have evolved to what were then unimaginable levels. Likewise, the banked, asphalt roads we travel today are just as far from the muddy trails on which the first bikes appeared; both have been through an incredible metamorphosis. Judging from its name, the boneshaker was a painful bike to ride. With a steam engine for propulsion, it was far from the fuel-injected, shock-absorbed, super-smooth bikes we have today. Roads went from muddy trails to gravel strips to wooden plank tracks to poured concrete interstates and are now ribbons of asphalt stretching cross-country like rivers flowing to the seas. All the while, motorcyclist are still searching for the perfect ride.

THE PERFECT RIDE

This book was written to help you find your perfect ride. Riders' preferences for road curvyness, scenery, and attractions are as far-ranging as their preferences for brands of motorcycles. Some riders might like hundreds of tight twists and turns while others don't want to work that hard. Finding a road that will please everyone might be impossible, but finding a region that will please everyone has been easy. In the area in and around western North Carolina, you'll surely find a ride that is pleasing to you. With beautiful scenery, comfortable accommodations, delicious food, and friendly natives, western North Carolina, east Tennessee, upcountry South Carolina, and southwestern Virginia are home to some of the best motorcycle adventures in the country.

MOUNTAIN ROADS

Because most of the rides in this book are in North Carolina, it might be useful for you to know a few things about the state's highway system. Since colonial times, North Carolina has been faced with the challenge of creating good roads in inhospitable conditions. With land ranging from swampland near the Outer Banks in the eastern part of the state to high mountain peaks in the west, the state has had a tough road to go. Road construction methods have changed through the years to meet the needs of the citizens. The first method converted Indian trails to "corduroy" roads. Corduroy roads were built by laying logs over the trails and covering them with branches and sand. Then came the plank roads.

These were built using wooden planks on which sand and gravel was spread. After that, several road improvement projects were commissioned in the state. No road project was as aggressive as the 1950s campaign known as the "Get the farmer out of the mud" program. Bridges from this road-building program still cross the rivers in the western part of North Carolina. Today, North Carolina boasts the largest state highway system in the country, with over 77,500 miles to maintain.

CHOOSING YOUR RIDE

With thousands of miles to explore, how will you ever find the road for you? This book lists 26 rides starting with brief descriptions. For each route, the ride overview describes what you'll see along the way— overlooks, restaurants, gas stations, attractions, and other cool stuff. You might find a ride that has the road conditions you like, but you don't have the time or the inclination to visit any of the sights along the way. You are in charge; just because something is mentioned doesn't mean you have to stop there. You might want to come back another day, but if you do want to stop, this guide will let you know what to expect.

THE BEST TIME TO GO

When's the best time to travel in the southern Appalachians? Well, this region is very mountainous and despite its low latitude, it has a high altitude. In the winter the higher elevations receive snowfall that remains on the ground all season. Many of the roads and businesses are seasonal due to the cold weather and inhospitable conditions. Other than the diehard alpinists, the riding season for most begins in early spring. After the roads open, watch for sand, gravel, and road salt left

over from snow-clearing. The spring is also when the many rhododendrons and mountain laurel bloom, creating a bright accent to dark green leaves. Midsummer is mighty hot in the rest of the south, but this region rarely reaches 90 degrees Fahrenheit. As a matter of fact, pack your leathers, even in July. Mornings can be downright chilly. In the fall, the temperatures begin to drop and the leaves explode into the colorful shades of autumn.

A WORD ABOUT
MY WORK ON THIS BOOK

Have you ever been out riding, seen a road and wondered where it went? Have you ever wondered if something was worth visiting? How about where to get a tasty meal? What if you could know for sure that the road ahead remains paved? Wouldn't it be nice to have a guy with you who would ride down that road, check it out and report back to you? Yeah? Well, I'm that guy.

Frequently, guidebooks are written with a bent toward businesses that support the author of the guide. My bank account can attest to the fact that not a single item in this book was paid for by anyone other than the publisher or me. Not a single campsite, no motel room, no meal, not even an admission to an attraction was given to me. Frankly, I didn't tell the businesses who I was. I didn't want them to know. That way, I got to experience them just as you will. So, how does a business show up in this book? If I see something that I would recommend to a friend, I've mentioned it. I hope you'll enjoy riding these mountain roads as much as I do, and I look forward to meeting you out there one day.

Code of the Road

There are written and unwritten laws, or "codes," that apply to the community of motorcyclists. Whether you are new to the sport or just rolled over one million miles, these codes help create a sport that is inviting to others, promotes camaraderie, and helps to keep us safe. What follows is a compilation of these written and unwritten laws, which many riders have come to know as the Code of the Road.

TYPES OF RIDERS & BIKES

Lean, throttle, clutch, brake, repeat. Those are your basic instructions for riding. Riders are funny about which parts of those instructions are their favorites. While the sportbikers enjoy the "lean," the cruisers among us enjoy the "throttle" a bit more than others. Touring riders tend to get a kick out of "repeat." Some bikers don't fit into the regular molds at all. I've seen a rider on a Gold Wing tearing through the Dragon as if she were on a ZX-9! On the other hand, I've seen a Ninja towing a trailer with a sidecar. It really doesn't matter what kind of bike you ride or what kind of biker you are, the point is that you belong to a greater community of riders.

CHOOSING A BIKE

Sure, the routes in this book could be enjoyed from a car, but why do that? Motorcycling offers so many choices. With hundreds of bikes made by dozens of companies, and aftermarket custom add-ons, the combinations are endless! Color, engine size, saddle comfort, speed, handling, noise, eye-catching looks, and ease of maintenance are all factors to consider when choosing a new bike. There's no "Best Bike." However, there is a "Best Bike for You." Ride what you like and like what you ride. Don't let anybody twist your arm to force you to buy a bike that isn't for you. Take your time. Finding a motorcycle is like finding a spouse: you learn from past dating experience what you like and dislike. You'll make choices based on your experiences. Some may like the simple pleasures offered by a 125cc dual-sportbike, while another biker will not settle for anything less than the sexy, slender curves of the hottest Italian model (I'm talking sportbikes here, guys!). Still others prefer a little extra weight for comfort for the long haul. There are as many different types of bikes as there are different types of people, and we are all linked by a thirst for adventure. It's more important that you ride, not what you ride.

JUSTIFYING YOUR RIDE

Why ride? Indeed, other than the fact that motorcycles speak volumes about how cool you are, there are some great reasons for riding—inexpensive initial cost, low operating costs, and the thrill of experiencing the open road. With used bikes priced from $500 to new hybrid models pushing the $100,000 mark, the initial cost is all about how much you have to spend. When gas prices rise, the motorcycle's excellent gas mileage becomes a sales boon. Like to see the scenery? A motorcycle has no doors and no roof to obstruct your view of the countryside. And another thing— bikes' "icebreaker appeal." No matter where you go on a bike, people are naturally drawn to it and to you. They may not show it, but all nonriders are envious. Deep down, everyone who doesn't ride looks back on a moment in time when they could have (or should have) gotten a bike or gone for a ride, but didn't. They have been plagued with the "what ifs" ever since. Give them something to talk about. Show them how cool you are by talking to them.

WAVING—AND WHY IT'S IMPORTANT

Other ways to demonstrate your coolness is by waving. Part of the camaraderie of motorcycling is a friendly wave to a fellow biker. Regardless of what make or model bike other riders are on, they are still cool enough to ride. Maybe it's because we share the dangers of the road, or because we are in on the secret of the natural high we get from our bikes, or hundreds of other reasons. Regardless, we wave. Just like commercial truck drivers talk on the CB, motorcyclists wave. There are many different kinds of waves used by motorcyclists. Here are a few I've run across over the years.

The "Point-and-Shoot Wave." This wave can be a little intimidating if you're on the receiving end, particularly if the sender is wearing dark gloves and is on the other side of an interstate. With the arm slightly bent, the first finger pointed toward the recipient and the thumb pointing straight up, then a "shooting" motion follows as the riders meet. Sometimes done with a flick, this wave has been credited to the famous Western movie star John Wayne and to a banking executive from Copper Hill, Tennessee (I'm deadly serious about the banking executive guy).

The "Right-Handed Wave." This wave accomplishes a couple of objectives all at once. First, it tells the recipient you're friendly and confident enough in your riding ability to let go of the handlebar to wave. Because you'll have to let go of the throttle to wave with your right hand, it also conveys

No matter how you do it, it's important (and fun) to wave to your fellow motorcycle riders.

that you have a great throttle lock, or cooler still, an electronic cruise control.

The "I'm #1 Wave." Ever popular, this one is indicated by an extended index finger pointed straight up. This wave resembles the dreaded "One-Finger Wave" which carries a less friendly meaning. Reserve the "One-Finger Wave" for those cars and trucks that creep over the center line in the tunnels along the Blue Ridge Parkway.

The "Hidden Hand Wave." This one is executed with the rider holding his hand down, palm facing the oncoming biker. It's hard to spot because the waving hand is covered by a black glove, which camouflages it in front of a dark background.

The "Invisible Wave." This one is used at night. Many riders instinctively wave despite the fact that it's way too dark out for the

oncoming rider to spot the raised hand. Oh, well, you get an "A" for effort if you use this wave.

STATE LAWS— A FACT OF LIFE

As unpopular as some of these may be, state laws were written in an attempt to protect you and others from evil and injury. If motorcyclists have one "hot button" topic to discuss, it's the helmet law. Wherever you fall on this topic, surely someone has asked your opinion or you have given your opinion freely. That's what America is all about.

What America is *not* all about is complaining to the messenger. What I mean by this is that if you get stopped by the local Constabulary for not wearing a helmet or doing something else that seems perfectly harmless (like speeding, passing on a double yellow line, or performing a cool wheelie) but is contrary to the state laws, you should expect a ticket. Giving the officer your opinion of the law won't help your cause and will only make the situation worse. If you really hate a law, even if it's one in another state, you can write to state legislators and let your complaint be heard by people who can change it. The elected lawmakers are sworn to hear your grievances about the laws they have created or failed to repeal.

Popular or not, here's a list of laws applying to motorcyclists for the Southern Appalachian states.

The surest way to get a ticket is to break the law. A double yellow line means no passing!

Summary of State Motorcycle Laws

LAW	VA	GA	NC	SC	TN
Helmets Required	Y	Y	Y	N[1]	Y
Eye Protection	Y[2]	Y[2]	N	N[1]	Y[2]
Daytime Headlight	N	Y	Y	Y	Y
Turn Signals	N	N	N	N	N
Rearview Mirror	Y	Y	Y	Y	Y
Headphones Permitted	Y	N[3]	Y	Y	Y
Max. Handlebar Height (above seat)	15"	15"	n/a	15"	15"
Brakes Front and Rear (f/r) Single (s)	f/r	s	s	f/r	s
Lane Splitting	N	N	N	N	N

[1] Required if under 21 years of age
[2] Not required if equipped with a windscreen
[3] Permitted only for communication

While there are certainly more laws relating to motorcycles than these, the most frequently questioned ones are listed here for convenient reference. This summary of state motorcycle laws was compiled by the author. This information was current as of July 2001.

NOTE: Virginia State Law prohibits the use or mere possession of radar detectors. North Carolina State Law allows police agencies to use unmarked vehicles for traffic enforcement.

Tips for the Road

DEALING WITH THE LAWMAN

A few years ago, I was a motorcycle police officer for the Cobb County Police Department in Metro Atlanta. Other than researching and writing motorcycle adventure guides, it was the greatest job I have ever had. They paid me money to ride a motorcycle. The training to become a motorcycle officer was extensive and difficult. The motorcycle-handling course had a large attrition rate. I attended the Police Academy and took extra courses in motorcycle safety and handling, weapons training, and various kinds of language training. I was no dummy. It's rare in this day and age to find an officer that is legitimately stupid.

Nowadays, most officers have college degrees. I didn't get into crime fighting for the money; I did it for the honor of serving the citizens I was sworn to protect. So, how do you think it went over when I stopped a helmetless biker and got a ticket thrown back in my face? Not well. My little biker buddy was complaining to the wrong man. I couldn't care less if he chose not to wear a helmet. But the state legislature cared enough to create a law. It was my job—duty, even—to enforce the laws they passed down to me. I explained to the guy that he needed to write a letter to the members of the legislative branch of government or take his case before the judicial branch of government, but arguing with the executive branch of government would only frustrate matters.

Somewhere, somehow, the motoring public lost sight of the fact that police officers are members of the same society to which they also belong. Some police officers have lost sight of this as well. In the unlikely event you do something that attracts the attention of an officer, you'll be better off if you remember that you are poured from the same mold that he or she was. So, what should you do when you meet a police officer? How do you get out of a ticket? There's no voodoo magic that always works, but here are some things that might help:

Show respect. I was amazed at how many people would cuss at me and talk bad about my momma and would then be shocked when I gave them a ticket. Believe me, you won't intimidate an officer with really nifty catch phrases and snappy comebacks. Disagreement is fine, but disrespect is unforgivable.

Talk, talk, talk. The longer the officer spends standing next to your bike, talking about *anything*, the less

Strike up a conversation with the officer. He's probably a nice guy.

anonymous you are to the officer. The better the officer knows you the less likely he will be to give you a ticket. Maybe something you'll say will remind the officer of Aunt Edna and he'll send you off with only a tongue-lashing. Let the officer in on what you've been doing and what your plans are. Show pictures, tell jokes, compliment the officer's uniform, do anything to keep the officer entertained for a minute or two.

Ask for a break. Nothing elaborate here. Try a simple, "Hey, Officer, I know you caught me red-handed when I passed you on that double yellow back there, but I didn't mean any harm. Besides, at 120 MPH it was hard to see the markings on your car. Could you please forgive me this indiscretion? Reduce the speed? Write a ticket for a nonmoving violation?" Often, the officer can issue you a ticket for a lesser speed, or even a nonmoving violation (such as a turn signal violation, or proof of insurance violation) that won't adversely effect your insurance rates.

Make the officer feel comfortable. Many officers have been killed doing exactly what the officer who stopped you is doing. Probably someone the officer has known or worked with has been killed while conducting a traffic stop. To lessen your chances of getting a ticket, let the officer know what you're going to do before you do it. Do not put your hands anywhere the officer can't see them (this includes the pockets of your pants and jacket). If you must do that to get your license, or registration or a photo of Aunt Edna, tell the officer what you are reaching for.

What about crying? What about it? Cry if you have to, but I was never impressed with it. Man or woman, I

never cared much for the show. An experienced officer will see through your charade like a pane of glass. The other tricks, like showing your bust line, flirting, and hiking up your skirt (on a motorcycle?), went out with disco. Sure, they are still used, but with limited success. The presence of video cameras in patrol cars, internal affairs investigations, and better training in police ethics make these tactics only an insult (albeit a humorous one).

So, you got a ticket—now what? Head to court on your assigned court date. Let's say you just want to pay the fine through the mail and be done with it. Paying through the mail might be convenient, but it's a guilty plea with the maximum fine. In court, you can meet with the prosecutor. The last thing the overworked prosecutor wants to do is fill up the court docket with simple speeding tickets. Still, be respectful in your arguments. If you see the officer, be polite to him too. The judge probably knows the officer, knows the officer's reputation for fairness, and will not look kindly on disrespect you show the officer, the prosecutor, or the court.

MURPHY'S LAWS OF MOTORCYCLING

I have no idea why this Murphy guy has such bad luck, but he sure does! Whether you've been riding for a lifetime or you just rolled the first ten miles onto your bike's odometer, you can expect the following laws to apply to you. Unlike state laws and lawmen, there's nothing you can do about Murphy's Laws. Nope, no amount of letter writing or roadside pleading will help. Once Murphy's Laws are put into motion, you just have to suffer through them. So try to prepare for them in advance, and be cool enough to laugh at them when they catch you.

Bike-falling-over Law: This law dictates that, magically, your bike will stand in your garage in front of you all by itself, without the use of a kickstand or any other means of support. However, once in the public eye, your bike will flop to the ground like a herring falling from a truck. (This happened to me as a motorcycle officer, when I stopped to change a tire for a group of college cheerleaders.)

Bike-breaking-down Law: You say something harmless-sounding to your buddies like, "I'm so glad I bought this bike, it's so reliable, never breaks down!" You can bet your last dollar that when you press the start button or try to kick it over, it will show no signs of life. Worse yet (this happened to me), you'll make fun of the reliability of someone else's bike and ride away on your trusty steed, only to break down later. Which leads to the:

Rider-stopping-to-help-you-will-make-you-endure-a-lesson-in-humility Law. You deserved it, now didn't you?

Rain Law: The weatherman has predicted cloudless skies and no rain in the entire region. You decide not to pack your rain gear. Of course the rain holds off until you're an hour from home, but when it hits (and it will) it's a deluge of biblical proportions.

Rain Gear Law: The sooner you stop to put on your rain gear, the sooner it will stop raining. Conversely, if you look up at the small rain cloud and decide to "ride it out for a minute," that little cloud will follow you and/or grow into a full-fledged thunderhead.

Loss-of-knowledge Law: Because you know the area you are planning to ride as if it were the back of your hand, you'll leave your map in the

Your friends said it was going to be a gentle ride. Murphy says otherwise.

garage. That's when the scenery will take your mind off the road and you'll become hopelessly lost. Every road you try seems to become a gravel driveway. This law also applies to maps drawn by friends telling you of a great ride.

Fuel Law: "I've got enough gas to make it to the next town." No you don't! Or the gas station in the next town will have burned during the morning biscuit-baking session.

ATM Law: ATM machines are great inventions. You can leave home with just two or three bucks in your pocket and use your ATM card when you need cash—or not! This law is usually applied to the riders who find themselves in a "Cash Only" establishment.

Cold Weather Law: You've planned a trip to the beach with your riding buddies and decide not to bring your warm riding leathers—after all, you're headed to the beach. It will snow at the beach.

Headlight Failure Law: Your headlight will only go out during a moonless night, dark thunderstorm, or long tunnel.

EQUIPMENT LIST

The effects of Murphy's Laws can be mitigated with some prior planning. To lessen Murphy's punch, find room for the following items:

A Small Tool Kit. You won't be doing a ring job, but tightening your chain or replacing a headlight bulb should be something you and your tool kit can handle.

Cash. Stash $50 in the tool kit. Leave it there until the ATM law strikes.

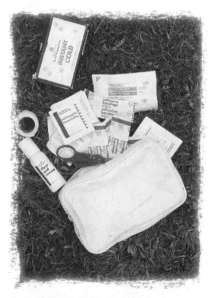

A good first aid kit is essential.

Rain Gear. It doesn't have to be fancy, just enough to keep it from raining.

Spare Headlight Bulb. Keep it wrapped in that bubble wrap stuff to prevent it from breaking.

Tire Repair Kit. Several companies make these with little CO2 cartridges to inflate a flat tire and plugs to make a temporary repair. It's temporary, but it beats being stuck in some remote location with a bike and a flat.

Other gear that's useful and will prevent or minimize small disasters:

First Aid Kit. Nothing elaborate, but equipped with what you'd need to keep a headache or a scrape from ruining your day.

A Passenger. To assist you when one of Murphy's Laws strikes.

Camera & Film. In the absence of a passenger, a great way to chronicle your adventure.

Tank Bag or Saddle Bags. To carry all this cool biker gear.

Baby Wipes. They'll freshen your face on a hot day or clean your hands after a chain-tightening.

Sting Ease. There are several products that ease the sting of insects.

Small Flashlight. Carry one big enough to light your bike long enough to change the headlight in the dark.

IMPORTANT PERSONAL GEAR

You. Are you rested and sober? Do you have a class "M" license? (Did you know that many single-vehicle motorcycle accidents are caused by riders who don't even possess a motorcycle license?)

Protective Gear. Helmet, gloves, long pants, jacket, glasses, and bright, "don't-run-over-me" clothing. Make sure your passenger is equipped with the same degree of protective clothing you are; the rider and

Traveling in groups is good, but leaving gear strewn about your bike and unattended is asking for theft.

passenger share the same degree of danger.

Sunscreen. No kidding—many riders don't think of this one, but as you sizzle in the tub after a weekend ride, you'll wish you had worn sunscreen.

PERSONAL SAFETY TIPS

As a police officer, I observed many people on vacation who seemed to feel that they were immune to crime and dropped their guard. Heck, you're on vacation! It's only natural for you to lower your guard. Criminals seem to be attuned to this phenomenon and take advantage of it. I don't want to make you paranoid; most people you'll meet will be just like you—on vacation and having a great time. Although small, your chance of becoming a crime victim is an unfortunate possibility. Here are a few things to consider to keep that chance to a minimum.

Most crimes are perpetrated against property, not people. Modern criminals don't want witnesses. They want your stuff and a clean getaway. And generally, they take whatever is convenient to take. So make getting your stuff a pain in the butt. If you do, the criminal will look for someone less prepared than you. Can your stuff be stolen, even with locks and all the crime prevention tools currently in use? Sure. For example, alarm systems keep most bikes from being stolen, but not all of them. There's no guarantee. Alarms are a deterrent, not a panacea.

Below is a brief list of tips I've recommended over the years:

Travel in groups. Criminals hate witnesses.

Be confident. Walk with your head up and look around, be observant.

Park in well-lit areas, away from vans (they block the view) and other large vehicles.

Lock your bike, even if you're at a scenic overlook and plan to be away from the bike for just a minute or two. My old Harley had a lock on the ignition switch. It was a pain to take out the little key all the time to lock it, but it was never stolen.

Use the handlebar lock. This is the one on your bike that you never use—you know, the one that's a pain in the butt. You have to turn the handlebar all the way to one side or the other and then turn the ignition key to a seemingly impossible position and pull it out. A word of caution: make sure your bike's taillight isn't illuminated (many bikes are equipped to turn on the taillight when the key is near this position). You don't want to kill your bike's battery!

Buy an additional lock, like the kind that fit on your front brake disk, or even a chain (get the rubber-coated chain so it doesn't ruin the finish on your rims).

Lock your gear, every time, every place. Break the habit of leaving your wallet in your saddle bag or under your seat. If it's convenient for you, it's convenient for the criminal.

At the motel or campsite: take the expensive stuff inside with you, and park as close to your motel door or tent flap as you can.

SOMETHING HAS HAPPENED. NOW WHAT?

Call the police immediately! 911 will work everywhere. Even if the county you're in has no 911 service, you'll be transferred to a county that does have a 911 system. If your nightmare has occurred on the Blue Ridge Parkway, call the Park Rangers at 1-800-PARKWATCH (that's 1-800-727-5928). Be prepared to give the responding officers your bike's description (including the make, model, tag number, V.I.N., and color). Ask the officer to put out a B.O.L.O. (cop lingo for Be On the Lookout) and have his records unit put your stolen bike on the N.C.I.C. (National Crime Information Center) right away. If the bike is seen by another officer, anywhere in the country, the computer will alert the officer that the bike is stolen.

Personal theft, like your gear or wallet, should be handled in a similar manner. As soon as the officer leaves, get on the phone and call your credit card companies. Cancel those cards before you pay for some criminal's sunny vacation in Miami! But to begin with, don't let the theft of your wallet be a trip-ender. Use the divide and conquer method—have extra money and/or credit cards stashed in different places. By keeping your eggs in several baskets, you still win if one of your baskets is stolen.

MAKE A LASTING IMPRESSION

There are no motorcycle etiquette police out on the open road. To help the sport flourish, it's up to us to present a good image of motorcycling. I'm not telling you to get rid of your beard or stop wearing black T-shirts, not at all. But, if someone was considering buying a bike and then saw the way you acted on yours, would they want to share the sport with you, or would your behavior push them away? Stay cool and ride safe!

The Asheville Area

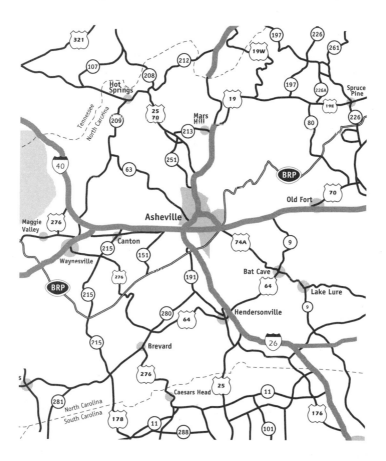

Much more than a grand city with a grand mansion, Asheville is surrounded by towering mountain peaks, quiet towns, and hundreds of miles of well-maintained roads.

Area Covered

*T*he founders of Asheville didn't know what motorcycles or motorcyclists were, but they somehow knew right where to build a city to provide the best roads and attractions for them. This big city with a little town feel is the gateway to western North Carolina. More than a convenient "jumping off point," Asheville offers much for the adventuring motorcyclist. Packed into Asheville are great places to stay, restaurants for every taste, and more to see and do than you'll be able to accomplish in a month.

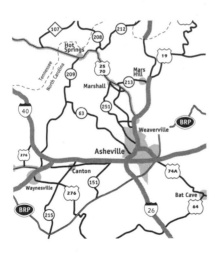

OVERVIEW

Unlike the other adventures in this book, this ride has no starting or ending point—it's just an overview of Asheville. Think of it as a "brass tacks" sort of motorcyclist's guide. With literally hundreds of places to eat and nearly as many attractions, information on Asheville could be the subject of this entire book. However, this is a regional motorcycle guide and not an unabridged tourist's guide to one town, so you won't find every single eatery and attraction here. I'm just scratching the surface.

On a map, Asheville can be found at the intersection of I-26 and I-40 on the banks of the French Broad River, in the center of western North Carolina.

PLACES TO SEE

In this section, you'll tour the Biltmore Estate and the Grove Park Inn (and car museum), and get an overview of the downtown area. There are lots of places to see and eat in Asheville. These few suggestions should keep you busy for a few days. Enjoy!

The **Biltmore Estate** is by far the most popular attraction in the city. You'll find it off US 25 just north of I-40 (exit 50). This largest private home in the U.S. was completed under the watchful eye of its owner, George Washington Vanderbilt III. Work began on the residence in 1889 and

GAS

Fuel is easily found throughout Asheville. Gas stations are particularly plentiful on Tunnel Rd. and near the Biltmore Estate.

employed about a thousand people during its six years of construction. It was completed in time for a Christmas party of mammoth proportions in 1895. This home was not only large, it was also technologically advanced. With amenities that included indoor plumbing, electricity, air conditioning, elevators, refrigerators and an indoor swimming pool, Biltmore was far ahead of its time. When completed, the residence employed 80 full time servants.

The Biltmore Estate got its name from the marriage of two words. "Bilt" from the Dutch town of Bildt, from whence Jan Aertsen van der Bilt came to America in the 1650s, and the English word *more*, meaning rolling farmland. Today, the Biltmore Estate stands open to the public.

The Vanderbilts made their fortune in the shipping and railroad businesses. They shared their wealth, too. A little college in Nashville called Central University became known as Vanderbilt University after the family donated $1,000,000 in 1873. The Metropolitan Opera in New York also benefited, as did the Medical School of Columbia University. Giving has always been an important part of the Vanderbilt family tradition.

Today, the Biltmore Estate is owned by descendants of George Vanderbilt III. William A.V. Cecil, G.W.'s grandson, has kept this beautiful home open and in nearly its original condition. The Cecils have added tasty amenities like a winery, several restaurants and even an ice cream parlor. You won't find any plastic tomahawks in the gift shop.

The basic entry package is $33. This includes a self-guided tour of the grand residence and formal gardens, plus a winery tour. If you feel like staying on the grounds, the Inn on Biltmore Estate offers luxurious accommodations. There are several large, satellite parking lots that shuttle tourists who arrive on four wheels to the front door of the mansion, but the Vanderbilts realized that motorcyclists are really cool people, so they allow us to park in

PHOTO BY HAWK HAGEBAK

To tour the Biltmore House itself, you'll need to park your bike and be prepared to do a bit of walking. Other than that, most of the rest of the estate is easily seen from two wheels.

The Asheville Area **21**

The massive Grove Park Inn is an impressive piece of architecture.

front of the residence. This is a superb photo opportunity for you and your bike in front of your "summer home."

For information on group rates (20 or more) and/or reservations, call 800-242-6480, or check out their website at www.biltmore.com. You can reach them by mail at Biltmore Estate, One North Pack Square, Asheville, NC 28801.

The **Grove Park Inn** is more than just a fancy old hotel. This 500-room inn was opened in 1913 by Edwin Grove. Construction took less than one year (11 months and 28 days, if you're counting). Mr. Grove used a design that was drawn by his nephew. This nephew had never designed anything, much less a hotel. Well, the old boy outdid himself, as the hotel has weathered the test of time. The same cannot be said of the relationship between Mr. Grove and the nephew. For reasons unknown to people outside the Grove family, they had a falling out and never spoke to each

other again. The Inn was used as an R & R center for the military after WW II. The military was a little rough on the Inn, but the place rebounded quickly.

Aside from its fascinating history, there are many attractions at the Grove Park. In the lobby, you'll see a gigantic fireplace and rock wall that was cut from a local crag. The rock was numbered as it was cut from the mountainside and put back together with exacting specifications to bring the cliff indoors. Outdoors, there's a great golf course that was refurbished in 2001 to the tune of $4,000,000. Back indoors, there are a couple of restaurants. The steakhouse won top honors in the City of Asheville in 2001. Another big draw to the hotel is the new spa, which was opened on February 28, 2001 with much fanfare. Its mudbaths and massage tables have not been empty since. If you are interested in the pampering offered at the spa, call ahead for reservations.

One less tangible attraction at the Inn is known as the Pink Lady. She is a friendly ghost who inhabits the Inn and makes things interesting for the guests and staff. Legend has it that the Pink Lady was a guest who fell (or was "assisted") from a high balcony. She never checked out. Guests have reported seeing her wandering the halls, entering rooms, and turning the lights on and off. She has never hurt or threatened anyone. She's the Pink *Lady*, and no *lady* would do harm to one of her guests.

You can reach the Grove Park Inn by calling 800-438-5800, or on the web at www.groveparkinn.com.

Next to the Grove Park Inn are the **Grovewood Shops and Museums**. Except for proximity, this small group of quaint buildings has nothing to do with the Grove Park Inn. It includes the Grovewood Cafe, the Grovewood Gallery, the Vanderbilt Industries

Interesting little bistros abound throughout downtown Asheville.

Museum, and an antique car museum. The Gallery is home to artwork that includes sculpture, paintings, and furniture. It costs nothing to browse. The Gallery is open seven days a week from 10 am to 6 pm, except Sunday when they open at 11 am. The Cafe offers great dining and outside seating Monday-Saturday from 11 am to 5 pm (opens at 1 pm on Sundays). Have a sandwich for about $7. The Vanderbilt Industries Museum chronicles the history of the textile business headed by Edith Vanderbilt. She used the carriage house buildings to house her clothing and balloon company. The antique car museum showcases about 20 antique cars and a few horse-drawn carriages. Sorry, no motorcycles on display, but maybe if we all say something to them, they'll change that. It costs nothing to tour the museums, but they politely ask for donations to the Cancer Society.

Reach the Cafe on the web at www.grovewoodcafe.com or by phone at 828-258-8956.

Downtown Asheville is a sight in itself. You can park your bike in one of many pay parking lots. *Biker's tip: When you park in one of these pay lots, arrive with a group of bikes and share the parking space. The attendants generally charge for the space, not the vehicle. Just make sure your friends don't stick you with paying for the space!*

Walk through the eclectic downtown area to the City/County Plaza. On weekend summer nights, you'll probably find folks gathered there enjoying bluegrass music and clogging, or other local performers showing their stuff to the crowd that usually shows up with blankets, wine, and cheese. Don't be surprised if you're asked to get up and square dance. They won't care if you don't have experience; instructors will help you through. Check out the many shops and restaurants. There are too many to mention here; you're sure to find something to suit your taste.

PLACES TO EAT

In two words: Tunnel Road. If you can't find something to your liking on Tunnel Rd., maybe you're just too darn picky! There's everything from **Carrabba's Italian Grill** to **Don Pablo's** Mexican. There's **Lone Star Steakhouse** and **Joe's Crab Shack** (where the wait staff frequently break into wild dancing and singing). If you're in a **Waffle House** mood, you'll find one of those on Tunnel Rd.

For more fancy dining, or more "locally known" dining, go through the tunnel on Tunnel Rd. and into downtown.

Downtown, Tunnel Rd. becomes College St. Continue straight into the heart of downtown and find a place to park. Downtown Asheville is very pedestrian-friendly, and all the really good stuff is within a few blocks from everything else.

Near the intersection of College St. and S. Lexington Ave. is the **Mediterranean Restaurant** (57 College St.). You will find it open every day except Sunday from 6 am to 4 pm. This is where the locals come for a great bite to eat. The owners imported their Mediterranean hospitality when they immigrated to Asheville from Greece. You'll get large portions for breakfast starting at just under $2, and a huge (so big you'll never finish it) seafood platter for $9.

Down Biltmore Ave. there are several great places to eat. There's a cafe offering outside dining on Pack Square. Not surprisingly, it's called **Cafe on the Square.** The phone number is 828-251-5565. Try **Barley's**

You might want to give the Cafe on the Square a try.

Taproom & Pizzeria just down the hill on Biltmore Ave. You'll enjoy a huge selection of well-brewed beers and equally well-crafted pizzas. You can give them a call at 828-255-0504. Another, more fancy-schmancy place to eat is the **Golden Horn Restaurant**, right next to Barley's. The **Golden Horn** is at 48 Biltmore Ave. and is open for lunch and dinner, offering great Italian fare. Call ahead for reservations for the Golden Horn at 828-281-4647. A very cool **double-decker bus** parked across the street from the Golden Horn and Barley's is actually a coffee shop. Stop in, get your coffee, climb to the upper deck, and watch the people pass by. If you are a coffee connoisseur, try **Beanstreets** at the intersection of College St. and Broadway Ave. Inside, you'll find more than a great cup o' joe; they serve sandwiches and pastries, too. Adorning the walls is the sometimes strange-looking work of local artists.

On the other side of College St., Biltmore St. becomes Broadway Ave. You'll find a **Mellow Mushroom** down the hill from College St. on the right. Mellow Mushroom is regionally famous for great pizzas with a hippie atmosphere. You can phone in your order so it will be ready when you arrive by calling 828-236-9800. For a taste of fine Japanese dining, try the **Heiwa Shokudo** restaurant at 87 Lexington Ave. near Hiawassee St. There's the **New French Bar** on Haywood Square at the intersection of Battery Park Ave. and Haywood St. With outside seating, one cannot help but imagine hearing a French accent. If you like Mexican or Caribbean food and lots of it, try **Salsa's** on Patton Avenue just down from the Square.

For a "biker bar," you'll have to leave town. There are two within 30 minutes of the city center. The **Do Drop In** in Black Mountain can be found by following Tunnel Rd. out of the city and toward Black Mountain. Tunnel Rd. is also US 70. Follow US 70 under I-240 and the Blue Ridge Parkway toward Black Mountain; from Asheville the ride will take only 15 minutes or so. The Do Drop In is on the left just as you enter the town of Black Mountain. Most nights you'll find lots of bikes of all makes and models parked out back. Inside, music flows from the mouths and guitar strings of local bands that aren't too famous—yet.

The **Margaritagrille** in Lake Lure is just a 30-minute ride from downtown Asheville. Follow US 74A (exit 53 from I-40) south toward Lake Lure, passing through the towns of Bat Cave and Chimney Rock. When you see the Lake Lure Marina on the left, the road bends to the right and the Margaritagrille will be on your right. You'll see plenty of bikes parked out front. They don't care what kind of bike you ride, only that you ride. The menu is southwestern, but the margaritas are said to be mind-numbing. Whether they are mindnumbing from the ice or the booze is up to you to decide; just don't drink and drive. The Margaritagrille is also a motel, and Lake Lure Inn is next door.

Pack Square, with its cool fountain, tall memorial, and pretty flowers, makes a great place to rendevous before taking in the sights of this city.

DIRECTIONS

To Biltmore Estate:
—From I-40, take exit 50.
—Go toward Asheville on US 25 and keep to the left.
—You'll fork to the left onto McDowell St. (still US 25) and then turn left into the estate entrance.
—There is a short ride to the reception center and then another couple of miles to the house.

To the Grove Park Inn:
—Take I-240 to exit 5B (Charlotte St.)
—After exiting, turn away from downtown Asheville.
—Go about .8 miles and turn right onto Macon Ave.
—Macon Ave. ends at the front door of the Grove Park Inn.

To the Grovewood Gallery, Cafe, and Museums:
—Follow the directions to the Grove Park Inn and then ride through the parking lot around back to find the Grovewood Gallery, Cafe & Museums.
—For a more scenic way to get there:
—Take exit 5B (Charlotte St.) from I-240 and turn away from downtown Asheville at the end of the ramp.
—Follow Charlotte St. about .3 miles down and turn left onto Edwin St. Follow Edwin St. to Country Club Dr. and turn right. Make another right onto Club View Dr. The Grovewood Gallery, Cafe, and Museums are at the dead end, in the shadow of the Grove Park Inn.

To Tunnel Rd. and Downtown Dining:
—Take exit 53 from I-40.
—At the bottom of the exit ramp turn north on I-240, which circles around the top of Asheville.
—Follow I-240 to exit 7 and take it. Turn left at the bottom of the exit ramp onto Tunnel Rd.
—After passing back under I-240 you'll be in the dining district.

Continue on Tunnel Rd. through the tunnel. Tunnel Rd. becomes College St., which cuts through the heart of downtown.

To Do Drop In:
—Follow Tunnel Rd. (US 70) out of Asheville, under I-240, past the V.A. Hospital, under the Blue Ridge Parkway and into the town of Black Mountain. The Do Drop In is on your left as you enter Black Mountain; motorcycle parking is around back.
—From I-40, take exit 55 and turn right (if you were westbound) or left (if you were eastbound). Follow that short stretch of road to US 70 and turn right. The Do Drop In will be on your left as you enter the town of Black Mountain.

To Margaritagrille:
—From I-40, take exit 53A onto southbound US 74A.
—Pass under the Blue Ridge Parkway and through the towns of Bat Cave and Chimney Rock. You'll see the Lake Lure Marina on your left as you enter the town of Lake Lure.
—Margaritagrille will be on the right side of the road, across the street from the Lake Lure beach.

Exploring Asheville

Legend:

75	Interstate Highway	28	NC State Highway	Route
27	US Highway	91	TN, VA, SC State Highway	Other Road
		5	Milepost	Blue Ridge Parkway

By far, this is the shortest and quickest ride featured in this book, and perfect if you have just a few minutes to get away. Consider it a "between-meals snack" for your bike. You'll enjoy great views of the growing Asheville skyline as you ascend the steep, well-paved and twisty road to the Blue Ridge Parkway, where you can ride a few sweeping curves and visit the Folk Art Center. From there, return by way of Tunnel Road, which cuts through a busy dining district—and Beaucatcher Mountain. It's a wonderful introduction to the city of Asheville and makes for a great escape into nearby mountains.

GAS

Gas is abundant on the last third of the ride on Tunnel Rd.

GETTING TO THE START

Start in downtown Asheville at the intersection of Tunnel Rd. (also known as College St., depending on which side of the intersection you are on) and Town Mountain Rd., on the downtown side of the tunnel. To get there from I-40, take exit 53 onto I-240 and follow that to exit 5B at Charlotte St. At the end of the ramp, turn left onto Charlotte St. and follow that just a couple blocks to College St., then make another left. Town Mountain Rd. will be on your left. Zero your trip meter as you turn onto Town Mountain Rd.

RIDE OVERVIEW

You'll begin this ride by turning off the four-lane Tunnel Rd./College St. onto the excellently paved and banked two-lane Town Mountain Rd. In the first quarter mile or less you'll leave the city behind and be greeted with beautiful homes and breathtaking views of Asheville. What's really cool is that you'll see the homes and the skyline at the same time, because the houses were built on the left side of the road and you have to look past them to see the skyline. So, you're killing two birds with one stone!

Just as your bike's tires are warm, you'll come to the end of Town Mountain Rd. and be greeted by the Blue Ridge Parkway. Once on the Parkway, enjoy the great sweeping curves that attract motorcyclists from all over the world. An overlook on the right side of the road gives a spectacular view of the Haw Creek Valley. From the overlook it's hard to believe you were in the city center just 15 minutes before!

Farther down the Parkway is the Folk Art Center. This unique center, open from 9 am to 5 pm every day, offers clean restrooms and information about the local area, but is best known for the local arts and crafts on display and for sale there. Most days you'll find a local artisan demonstrating his or her craft in the lobby. You might see someone throwing pots, painting, or even quilting. Much of what is on display is also for sale.

About a half mile past the Folk Art Center is the ramp to US 70 west. US 70 west is also known as Tunnel Rd. You'll ride down the ramp onto Tunnel Rd. Follow Tunnel Rd. west past the V.A. Hospital, Scooter Tramps Custom Motorcycle Parts, and under I-240. Just remember to stay to the left as you near I-240, because the right lane merges onto I-240 and this ride continues straight. Soon after

TOTAL DISTANCE
16 miles

TIME FRAME
30 minutes, but that doesn't include any time you'll need to visit the Folk Art Center on the Blue Ridge Parkway or to dine in one of the many nationally franchised eateries on Tunnel Rd.

passing under I-240, Tunnel Rd. gets mighty busy. There are many places to eat and stay on this section of the ride. If the allure of the nationally franchised eateries doesn't appeal to you, ride through the tunnel and into the downtown section.

The ride ends where it began, just on the downtown side of the tunnel.

Downtown Asheville offers much to the motorcyclist. With great sidewalk cafes and coffee shops and a boatload of attractions, you're sure to enjoy the little town feel of the city of Asheville. Check out the *Exploring Asheville* chapter for more information about downtown.

Asheville lies in the French Broad River valley that splits the Blue Ridge. Enjoy the views of the city as you ascend Town Mountain Rd.

RIDE ALTERNATIVES

When the ride turns off the Blue Ridge Parkway onto Tunnel Rd., you don't have to! You can continue a few more miles south to reach US 74A, which will lead you to Lake Lure, or you can follow the Parkway all the way to Cherokee (plan about six hours for that ride).

ROAD CONDITIONS

Quiet, two-lane, excellently paved and banked, Town Mountain Rd. and the Blue Ridge Parkway are a pleasure to ride. Tunnel Rd. is not quiet. Rather, it is a busy four-lane (and sometimes six-lane) piece of city roadway. Watch for cars turning into and coming out of the many businesses that line both sides of Tunnel Rd. Remember, Tunnel Rd. gets its name from a tunnel. As you ride through that tunnel, keep to the right half of your lane to prevent a head-on collision with a passing motorist.

POINTS OF INTEREST

Asheville Skyline, Blue Ridge Parkway, Folk Art Center, many national franchise restaurants, Beaucatcher Tunnel on Tunnel Rd.

RESTAURANTS

Name your favorite restaurant—there's probably one of those on Tunnel Rd. With literally dozens of choices, Tunnel Rd. will have what you're looking for. Here's a very partial list: **Don Pablo's, Joe's Crab Shack, Rio Bravo, Lone Star Steakhouse, Applebee's, fast food**, and of course a **Waffle House**. There are also dozens of motels and hotels on Tunnel Rd. The biker favorite (and one of the cheapest) is the **Mountaineer Inn**. Never mind the fact that the double E's in the word Mountaineer are backwards.

DETAILED DIRECTIONS

MILE 0—Turn off Tunnel Rd./College St. onto Town Mountain Rd. (also known as NC 694). *Follow the twists and turns up the mountain and look to your left over and around the opulent homes to catch glimpses of the Asheville skyline.*

MILE 6.4—Town Mountain Rd. ends into the Blue Ridge Parkway; turn right. *At mile 8.9, you can enjoy a view of the Haw Creek Valley from an overlook. Pay a visit to the Folk Art Center at mile 11.*

MILE 11.4—Turn right off the Parkway and onto the access ramp to US 70 west/Tunnel Rd. At the bottom of the ramp, turn right onto US 70 west/Tunnel Rd. *Move to the left lane and remain there to avoid being swept onto I-240 which takes the right lane of Tunnel Rd. at mile 13.7. You'll enter the bigtime dining and lodging district at mile 14.5. At mile 15.5, the ride takes you through Beaucatcher Tunnel and into the business district of downtown Asheville.*

MILE 16—The ride ends where it began. *Continue straight onto College St. to see what the downtown area offers, or ride back through the tunnel to check out the dining district.*

City Escape

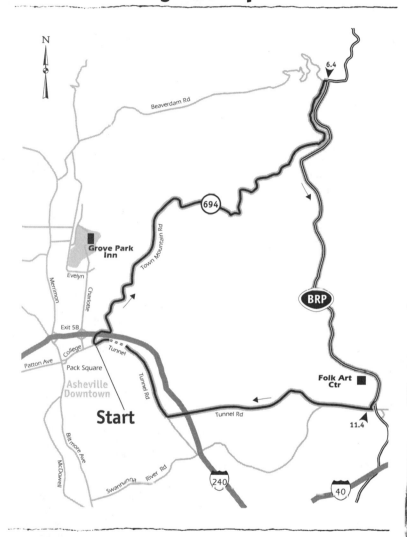

N

Beaverdam Rd

6.4

694

Grove Park Inn

Town Mountain Rd

Evelyn

Merrimon

Charlotte

Exit 5B

College

Patton Ave

Tunnel

Pack Square

Asheville Downtown

Start

Tunnel Rd

Tunnel Rd

BRP

Folk Art Ctr

11.4

Biltmore Ave

McDowell

Swannanoa River Rd

240

40

75   Interstate Highway

27   US Highway

28   NC State Highway

91   TN, VA, SC State Highway

5 ▶   Milepost

 Route

Other Road

 Blue Ridge Parkway

Lake Lure Run

This is a quick ride to and from Asheville. It offers nice roads, good scenery, and lots of activities. Maybe you'll choose to take a short hike up Chimney Rock, or rent a boat on Lake Lure, maybe visit the "bottomless pools," or just settle into a bar chair at the Margaritagrille, one of the best biker bars in the region. If you take this ride once, you'll be hooked forever.

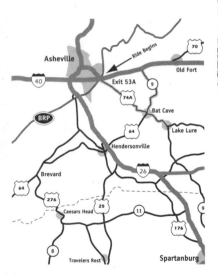

GETTING TO THE START

You'll begin this route just a half mile from I-40, exit 53A on US 74A. Reset your trip meter as you pass under the Blue Ridge Parkway.

RIDE OVERVIEW

Begin under the Blue Ridge Parkway on US 74A south, heading toward Chimney Rock and Lake Lure. That's just .5 miles off I-40 (exit 53A). To get there, you can take either I-40 or the Blue Ridge Parkway. While I-40 is more direct, the Parkway offers great views, twists, and turns.

US 74A has been under construction for the past few years as the DOT has decided to widen it. Don't despair, there are curves aplenty ahead for you. As a matter of fact, at mile 9 of this ride the road begins a series of hairpin turns that lead you to the Eastern Continental Divide at 2,880 ft. above sea level. What's the Eastern Continental Divide? On one side of the mountain, falling rain flows to the Atlantic Ocean; rain falling on the other side of the same mountain flows to the Gulf of Mexico.

Descending toward Chimney Rock and Lake Lure, you'll pass through the little town of Bat Cave. It gets its name from the largest fissure cave east of the Mississippi, which is said to be full of bats. Sorry, public tours of the cave ended years ago, but researchers go there frequently to study the cave's unusual geological features and its abundant wildlife.

Public tours *are* permitted and encouraged at Chimney Rock. This beautiful and privately maintained 1,000-acre park offers superb views of Lake Lure, the town of Chimney Rock, the surrounding mountains, and the 404 ft. cascade of Hickory Nut Falls. From US 74A in downtown Chimney Rock, the ride to the Chimney Rock visitor center is paved and extremely twisty. From the visitor center, an elevator will take you up the equivalent of 26 stories and leave you near the summit of Chimney Rock. From there, it's just a short hike to the unusual outcropping from which the park gets its name. After you take in the views from Chimney Rock, try out the 45-minute hike to Hickory Nut Falls.

Back on the ground, you'll find many shops and restaurants. One of the coolest shops in Chimney Rock is the Heavenly Hoggs motorcycle accessory store. Your collection won't be complete without a T-shirt from this shop. And restaurants? This place is home to more restaurants than you could visit in a week.
From North Carolina barbecue to northern European fare, there's something here for everyone. Or, plan a dinner cruise on Lake Lure.

Lake Lure Tours offers sunset dinner cruises to one of several lakeside restaurants. Better plan ahead; the dinner cruises are popular and reservations fill up fast. Lake Lure Tours can be found on the web at www.lakelure.com or reached by phone at 828-625-0077. If a guided tour of Lake Lure's 27-mile shoreline doesn't suit you, you might want to go it alone by renting a pontoon boat. Again, call head to reserve one. Regardless, try to get out on the lake during your visit. The views of the mountains are enhanced by the lake's clean, blue expanse of water.

TOTAL DISTANCE
43 miles

TIME FRAME
1½ hours from start to finish. Add time for stops if you're going to visit Chimney Rock, tour Lake Lure or, have a cold one at Margaritagrille.

Let's say you hate boating, and aren't fond of heights. At least take advantage of the Lake Lure boardwalk that runs about a quarter mile from the marina to the beach. Once at the beach you're sure to spot the Margaritagrille, where margaritas and Tex/Mex are the house specialties. This little bar hosts several hundred visiting motorcyclists every weekend night. The house really gets rocking on Friday and Saturday nights when the band is playing. If you have a little too much to drink and don't want to crash your bike on the way back to Asheville, you can stay at the motel right there at the bar or you might decide to take advantage of the luxury accommodations of the Lake Lure Inn, a short crawl away.

Lake Lure Inn opened in 1927 and has played host to guests ranging from F.D.R. to Patrick Swayze. With its 50 rooms and deluxe dining, this hotel has earned its nickname, "the Little Waldorf of the South."

Near the hotel is the driveway to the Bottomless Pools. These pools were made famous after being mentioned in Ripley's Believe It or Not. The owners of the three pools have built a covered bridge leading to the $3-per-person toll booth and then on to the bottomless pools. It's touristy, but who cares?

The route makes a U-turn at the gas station near the edge of town. From the gas station, Murry's Tavern is close by. To be honest, nothing is far from anywhere in Lake Lure. Murry's offers food and drink without the raucous sounds of Margaritagrille.

As you ride back through the towns of Lake Lure and Chimney Rock, keep an eye out for that perfect souvenir you missed on the way in. The ride makes a right turn in Bat Cave.

In "downtown" Bat Cave, you'll be turning right onto NC 9. NC 9 is a well-paved and excellently banked stretch of road that spins and twists you back over the Eastern Continental Divide on your way to the town of Black Mountain.

The ride ends at the intersection of I-40 and NC 9. Go west on I-40 for a ten-minute ride back into Asheville, or head east a few miles to get to the beginning of the Little Switzerland Loop.

RIDE ALTERNATIVES

If you just want to ride and care nothing about seeing Chimney Rock or Lake Lure, avoid both of them by turning left onto NC 9 from US 74A at mile 17.2. That will shorten the ride by nearly nine miles, but you'll lose nothing in the way of great riding.

ROAD CONDITIONS

US 74A can be a little rough. While some stretches have been under construction for years, other parts of the road have remained untouched by DOT crews for years. With cracks and the occasional pothole, US 74A deserves your full attention. NC 9, on the other hand, is an excellent piece of asphalt. It's freshly paved and well banked; you're sure to enjoy it. Chimney Rock and Lake Lure traffic can be mighty heavy on summer weekends, so keep

your head up and watch for folks pulling out of the roadside parking areas.

POINTS OF INTEREST

Chimney Rock Park, Lake Lure (tours and boat rentals), the Bottomless Pools, the historic Lake Lure Inn, and Margaritagrille.

RESTAURANTS

While there are so many restaurants in Chimney Rock and Lake Lure that they could be the subject of an entire book, two of them really stand out. **Margaritagrille** in Lake Lure offers Tex/Mex cuisine and drinks galore. With a band every weekend night, the place is an excellent biker hangout. **Murry's Tavern** offers quieter fare with burgers and suds dominating the menu.

DETAILED DIRECTIONS

MILE 0—Begin on US 74A southbound under the Blue Ridge Parkway. *At mile 9, be ready for the curves. The Eastern Continental Divide sits at mile 11.2. You can enter Chimney Rock Park near mile 19.5. Lake Lure Marina with its guided tours and boat rentals is at mile 21.3. Also at mile 21.3 is Margaritagrille, and just around the corner is the Lake Lure Inn. You'll find the driveway to the Bottomless Pools at mile 21.5. Murry's Tavern is close by.*

MILE 21.6—Make a U-turn at the gas station on the far side of the Lake Lure Beach.

MILE 25.9—Turn right onto NC 9 in Bat Cave heading toward the town of Black Mountain.

MILE 43—The ride ends at the junction of NC 9 and I-40.

Lake Lure Run

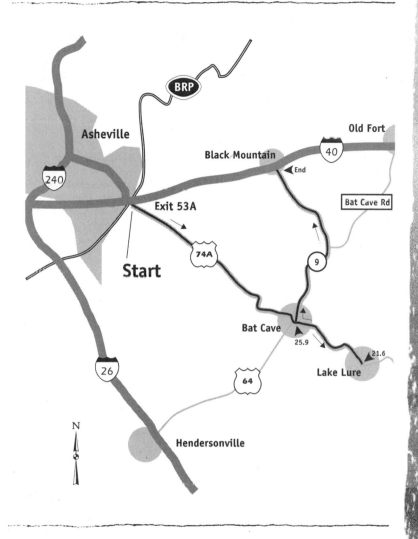

Asheville

BRP

Old Fort

Black Mountain

◄End

40

Bat Cave Rd

240

Exit 53A

74A

9

Start

Bat Cave

25.9

21.6

Lake Lure

26

64

Hendersonville

N

75	Interstate Highway	28	NC State Highway	▬▬ Route
27	US Highway	91	TN, VA, SC State Highway	— Other Road
		5▶	Milepost	▬▬ Blue Ridge Parkway

*I*f riding through a landscape reminiscent of the Scottish Highlands on twisty mountain roads, passing through small towns, and dining in the lap of luxury sound good, this adventure is for you. "But wait, there's more!" I exclaim. Once in Hot Springs, you can take in an adrenaline-pumping river run, soak in a tub fed by the natural hot springs, or do both and then top it off with a massage. The surrounding lush green landscape provides the perfect setting for a restful and relaxing day—or an entire weekend.

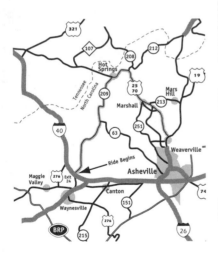

GAS

Gas is available at the start and at miles 8.1, 18.4, 33.2, 45.5, 46, 49.4, 51, and 59.4.

GETTING TO THE START

This ride starts about 25 minutes west of Asheville on NC 209 off I-40 at exit 24. After exiting, zero your trip meter as you head north on NC 209.

RIDE OVERVIEW

When you begin this ride off I-40 on NC 209 north it will seem like you're about 1,800 miles across the ocean—no longer in North Carolina, but rather in Scotland. The lush green rolling hills, home to sheep, goats, and cattle, are punctuated by granite boulders much like those highland hills. If you allow yourself to imagine, you might just hear the haunting melodies of bagpipes wafting through the valley. It's not surprising Scottish settlers were drawn to this region.

NC 209 makes a right turn at Ferguson Supply. Inside Ferguson's you'll find nearly anything you might need. It's an old country general store without the "old" stuff. They offer fuel, food, and dry goods, including fishing and hunting supplies.

After turning at Ferguson's, NC 209 becomes less like Scotland and more like an amusement ride. The many climbs, dips, and twists give the feeling of riding a roller-coaster. You'll still encounter a couple of straightaways, but bear in mind that these are nearly always followed by an unmarked sharp bend in the road. With a little bit of skill and luck you'll do just fine.

You'll be in Luck about 17 miles into the ride. No, this is not the same kind of luck you need at the slots in Cherokee, NC; this is the town of Luck. There is but one business in Luck and you'll be lucky to find it open. It used to be a gas station, but now sells local artwork and antique knickknacks. A photo with the "Luck" sign is a must for your motorcycle scrapbook. Continuing north on NC 209, you'll be out of Luck, but you'll find Trust a few miles ahead.

In Trust you'll find the Trust General Store (with fuel) and the Spring Creek Cafe. The Trust General Store replaced the Ebbs and Gardner General Merchandise Store that served the area from 1900 until the 1950s. The old ledger from Ebbs and Gardner is on display in the Spring Creek Cafe. You're invited to gently leaf through the pages of the old ledger to see how the mountain residents used to barter and trade for nearly anything. It's interesting to compare 1902 prices to 2002 prices! Wow, they had it good!

Snap a photo to prove you were once in Luck.

Other than being a mini-museum for the towns of Trust and Luck, the Spring Creek Cafe offers great meals at super prices. Serving lunch and dinner everyday except Monday, the cafe is sure to have something on the menu for you. Lunch prices range from $1.50 to $6 with over 15 sandwich and salad choices. The dinner menu is a bit more costly with prices from $8 to $14, but you'll get a meal that could stuff a small army. After moving your belt to the next notch to accommodate the delicious meal you just had, continue north on NC 209.

You'll follow Spring Creek as it winds its way north under a canopy of trees. Any motorcyclist will appreciate the cooling effect of water and trees on a hot summer day. It's like air conditioning. The road turns away from Spring Creek and heads up the side of a steep mountain slope. This is your introduction to the Spring Creek Gorge. There are three gravel overlooks that offer great views of the gorge below. Watch for loose gravel that has spilled onto the roadway. Another thing to watch for is the town of Hot Springs just past the gorge—you'll be there before you know it.

Hot Springs is a small town with a population of around 1,000. Don't let

On the road to Hot Springs, you'll pass many a mountain farm. Keep a lookout for slow-moving machinery.

its small size lull you into thinking that it has little to offer. This hamlet packs a powerful punch, full of adventure! Hot Springs hosts several motorcycle rallies each year. Also in Hot Springs, the end of NC 209 meets US 25/70. You'll continue straight onto US 25/70.

As you enter Hot Springs, you may notice a lot of hikers walking down the sidewalk. The Appalachian Trail crosses through the middle of town. At the Smoky Mountain Diner, hikers enjoy hot meals at a reasonable price. Open for breakfast, lunch, and dinner, the diner offers food and prices similar to the Spring Creek Cafe (only the Smoky Mountain Diner is open for breakfast). Farther down the Appalachian Trail are other dining establishments.

Dining in Hot Springs is all about choices. You can eat at the Smoky Mountain Diner or try the more upscale restaurants down the street. Depending on how fancy you care to get and how much money you have to spend, you might want to consider the Paddler's Pub or the Bridge Street Cafe.

At the Paddler's Pub you'll find huge cheeseburgers served with chips or homemade potato salad and a beer for about $10.50, or a steak dinner with a glass of wine for about $18-$20. As the name implies, they serve beer and wine at this restaurant—*lots* of different kinds of beer. For real adventure, try the local microbrew, the "Goldenrod Lager," brewed by the French Broad Brewery. Open for lunch and dinner, it's a gathering place for locals, French Broad paddlers, passing hikers, and coolest of all, motorcyclists.

The Bridge Street Cafe and Inn is a little more expensive and a little more formal. Open for dinner Thursday through Sunday, this gem of a restaurant offers delicious gourmet meals prepared by a chef from Louisiana. The chef gives nearly every dish a French accent. You can dine in opulent comfort on the flower-covered deck overlooking Spring Creek. From pizzas to pasta, steak to salmon, there's something for everyone in nearly every price range. You can spend from $10 to $100. There's an extensive wine and beer list, too. If you've had too much to drink, stay at the inn upstairs. Dinner and lodging reservations are strongly recommended.

Now that you've eaten, it's time for an adrenaline rush. For real adventure, paddle down the rapids of the French Broad River. There are many outfitters, but the Nantahala Outdoor Center (NOC) and USA Raft outfitters are the most popular. The French Broad

Outpost of the NOC offers half-day (with or without lunch) and full-day trips. If you are considering this adventure, you'll need to make reservations by calling NOC at 800-232-7238, or find them on the web at www.noc.com. There are many smaller outfitters offering rafting trips of various lengths and costs. You might want to shop around for the best deal.

Let's check our list again. You've ridden, eaten, and gotten an adrenaline rush—now it's time to take care of those muscles made sore by the ride and the whitewater adventure. Just over the train tracks in downtown Hot Springs is the entrance to the Hot Springs Spa.

At the Hot Springs Spa, the springs feed 100-degree water into modern and comfortable hot tubs. While there are many spas to choose from, #5 and #6 offer the most privacy. They cost just $15 an hour per couple before 7 pm; after that it's just $25 an hour per couple. If the warm spring water doesn't take care of all your sore muscles, the Hot Springs Spa has massage therapists on staff to get rid of that soreness once and for all.

If you decide there's too much to do in Hot Springs in just one day, you can stay at the Hot Springs Spa. The Spa offers camping ($10), primitive cabins ($41), and cabins with restrooms ($55-60). Or, go all out and get the deluxe cabin ($128) with all the comforts of home. The deluxe cabin sleeps four and comes complete with its own private spa for you to enjoy as long as you like. Reservations for the spas, massages, and cabins are recommended. For information call 828-622-7676. The web address is www.hotspringsspa-nc.com.

Continuing south on US 25/70, you'll take in some sweeping curves as you head toward a "T" intersection. At this intersection, the adventure turns right, but you can add more riding to your day by turning left onto NC 208 and taking in the northern part of the Buncombe Turnpike Ride.

Turning right and staying on US 25/70 south, you'll roll through the countryside as you head toward Asheville. US 25/70 becomes a four-lane divided highway along the way. The ride ends where US 25/70 meets US 19/23 south.

RIDE ALTERNATIVES

You can add some great twists and turns to your riding day by turning left onto NC 208 at mile 38.6 and adding the last half of the Buncombe Turnpike ride (p. 52) to this adventure. If you want to start your adventure in Hot Springs, ride this route in reverse.

Finish off your ride in style with a soak at the Hot Springs Spa.

ROAD CONDITIONS

NC 209 is a two-lane, well paved and adequately banked chunk of traffic engineering. However, there is a lack of signage to warn you of approaching tight turns. It's best to assume that the road ahead is going to twist. Occasionally, the gravel from the scenic overlooks along the Spring Creek Gorge makes its way to the road, creating a hazard. In Hot Springs, watch for pedestrians as the Appalachian Trail makes its way down the sidewalk of Main St.

US 25/70 is a wide, two-lane road that becomes a four-lane divided highway which rolls effortlessly toward Asheville.

POINTS OF INTEREST

The Scottish Highlands-like valley at the adventure's beginning, the towns of Luck and Trust, the Spring Creek Gorge, the Hot Springs Spa, the French Broad River, several great restaurants, and the Appalachian Trail.

RESTAURANTS

In Trust is the **Spring Creek Cafe**, offering lunch and dinner at good prices. With lunch items from $1.50 and dinner items starting at just $7.95, you're sure to find something to please your palate *and* your wallet.

In Hot Springs, you can choose from a classic diner to more gourmet options. For the former, try out the **Smoky Mountain Diner**, offering hot breakfast, lunch, and dinner. For more cosmopolitan fare, try the **Bridge Street Cafe & Inn**. This restaurant offers delicious Mediterranean and organic dishes from $10 to $25. To complement your meal, the cafe serves up wine and beer along with live local music. To book a room or to make dinner reservations, call 828-

622-0002, or check in with them on the web at www.bridgestreetcafe.com. The best burger in town can be found at the **Paddler's Pub**. As the name suggests, you can get a beer there, or enjoy a glass of wine. Dinner at the Paddler's Pub includes steak, seafood, and other popular dishes. For a real beer-drinking adventure, try the Goldenrod Lager, a local brew.

DETAILED DIRECTIONS

MILE 0—Turn north on NC 209 from I-40 (exit 24). *Enjoy the sweeping curves through scenery resembling the Scottish Highlands.*

MILE 8.1—Turn right to stay on NC 209. *Ferguson Supply is at this intersection.* **Use caution for the next several miles;** *without warning, the road twists wildly. You'll be in Luck at mile 16.9. In Trust at mile 18.4, you'll find the Trust General Store and the Spring Creek Cafe.*

MILE 26.7—NC 209 forks to the right. *Between mile 29 and 31 there are three gravel overlooks of the Spring Creek Gorge. You'll enter the town of Hot Springs near mile 32.5.*

MILE 33.2—The Smoky Mountain Diner is at mile 33.2. Hwy 209 ends here; continue straight onto US 25/70. *The Paddler's Pub and the Bridge Street Cafe are next door neighbors at mile 33.5. On the left at mile 33.6 is the Hot Springs Spa & Campground.*

MILE 38.6—Turn right to stay on US 25/70. *US 25/70 becomes a four-lane highway at mile 51.4.*

MILE 59.8—The ride ends where US 25/70 and US 19/23 meet. *To head toward Asheville and I-40, take the exit onto US 19/23 south.*

Hot Springs

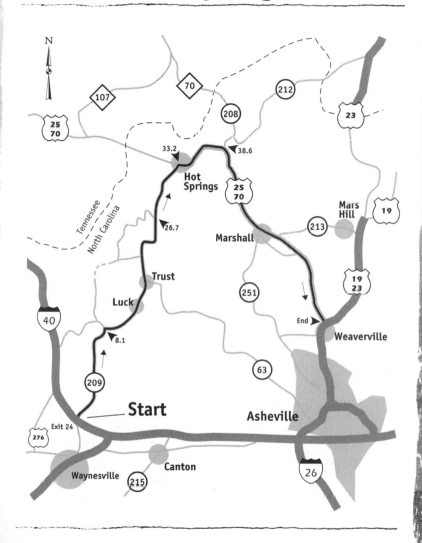

T rust your instincts on this route. With great surface conditions and little traffic, you're sure to enjoy the ride up and over Doggett Mountain as well as through several small villages and farmsteads. Luck will be on your side all day. As a matter of fact, you'll be passing through Trust and Luck. Not only has the state of North Carolina produced some beautiful roads, it also has some quaint towns with very interesting names. Besides, who doesn't have fun thinking of clichés that include trust and luck?

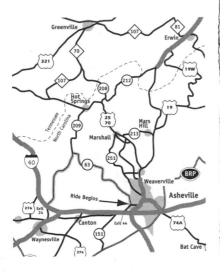

GAS

Gas is available at the start and along the first 4.5 miles, then at miles 8.1, 10, 15.4, 27.5, 37.6, and at the ride's end.

GETTING TO THE START

This ride starts in Asheville on US 19/23 at NC 63 west. To get there from I-40, take exit 44 on I-40 and turn north onto business route US 19/23. You'll find NC 63 on the left in about three miles. Reset your trip meter as you turn west onto NC 63.

RIDE OVERVIEW

From Asheville, the route at first is straight and commercial. Trust me, it gets better. In fact, this five-lane road becomes a two-lane state route in just 4.5 miles. Along NC 63 you'll spy lots of old farmsteads as well as some new businesses. The town of Leicester is home to many old Victorian homes that are plainly visible from the road.

From Leicester, NC 63 begins to roll and sweep through the countryside. Along the way, you'll pass many cattle and goat farms. Speaking from experience, I recommend you watch your speed on this section. A collision with a wandering farm animal would end your adventure much too soon.

Beyond the livestock, NC 63 begins its ascent up Doggett Mountain. A four-mile series of tight twists provide the interest here because there's little in the way of scenic views from NC 63.

There is one spectacular view from atop Doggett Mountain, where a small dirt driveway on either side of the road offers some space to pull off and take a rest. On weekends, you'll likely find bicyclists taking in this view while catching their breath.

Descending Doggett Mountain is much like climbing it—steep and twisty. You'll find a few small farms on this side of the mountain, but nothing like those on the Asheville side. Soon, you'll come to St. Jude's Chapel of Hope on the left (mile 27.2).

St. Jude's Chapel of Hope was opened in June of 1991. It was built to give passersby a quiet place to contemplate, meditate, or pray. You need not be religious to enjoy this chapel's appeal. Small but well appointed, its pews seat just eight people, and the stained glass and interior details make it very pleasant. No regular services are held in the chapel, but it is always open.

At the end of NC 63, turn left onto NC 209. Right there in downtown Trust, NC, is the Trust General Store which houses the Spring Creek Cafe and a gas station-store combo. Great prices, delicious meals (lunch and dinner only), and friendly servers make the cafe a favorite destination. The history of Trust is on the menu and the walls of the cafe. The old general store's ledger offers a glimpse into the past.

Just past the General Store a plaque on a small covered bridge proclaims, "Bridge of Madison County." This is not the bridge from the Clint Eastwood movie. However, you *are* in Madison County and it *is* a covered bridge, so make up your own road lie and go with it.

Up ahead is a little bit of Luck—a very little bit. Luck, NC, is little more than a sign. The one shop in Luck used to be a gas station. Its rusting antique pumps let you know that there's no gas in Luck; it now offers

TOTAL DISTANCE
46 miles

TIME FRAME
1 hour from start to finish.
Add time to eat in Trust, or to visit St. Jude's Chapel of Hope.

antique trinkets and samples of local artwork. You're lucky if you find it open.

So, you've got Luck and Trust. Need Faith? Reverend Hightower invites you to the Lusk Chapel for a country service. You'll find the Lusk (not to be confused with Luck) Chapel on the left side of the road just a mile or so out of Luck.

NC 209 continues its twisty journey westward. There are some straight-aways on NC 209, but be forewarned that coming up are horrendous curves up or down a mountain. These will be replaced by rolling sweepers as you near the end of the ride.

At a "T" intersection, you'll see Ferguson's Supply on the right. Like general stores of old, Ferguson's has nearly anything you might need, or think you might need—gas, groceries, ice cream, and even a little restaurant.

Make a left at Ferguson's to remain on NC 209 and you'll begin to see why Scottish Highlanders felt at home and settled here. With its lush green hills and granite outcroppings, it looks much like Scotland.

The ride ends at the intersection of NC 209 and I-40. Go east on I-40 to return to Asheville or continue south on NC 209 to head toward Waynesville and on to US 74 west to Murphy.

RIDE ALTERNATIVES

This ride is very close to the Hot Springs ride (p. 36), and actually overlaps part of the route. Once in Trust, if you decide to venture into Hot Springs, turn right instead of left onto NC 209 from NC 63. In doing so, you'll be out of Luck (Luck, NC, that is).

ROAD CONDITIONS

The first 4.5 miles of NC 63 are straight and highly commercialized. Traffic is heaviest here, too, so watch for cars pulling out of the many businesses that line both sides of the road. NC 63 and NC 209 are excellently paved and banked, and are generally free of debris. They do lack signage. It seems that the twistiest parts of this route occur in thick woods, after a long straightaway.

POINTS OF INTEREST

Doggett Mountain, St. Jude's Chapel of Hope, the Bridge of Madison County, the towns of Trust and Luck.

RESTAURANTS

There's one great place to eat on this ride. In Trust, you can dine in the **Spring Creek Cafe**. It offers lunch and dinner every day except Monday, when it is closed. The lunch menu is covered with salads and over 15 different kinds of burgers and sandwiches, all served with chips (fries are 50 cents extra). Lunch is priced from $1.50 to $6. Dinner is a bit more costly, but you get what you pay for. Heaping helpings of seafood, beef, pork and chicken make up the dinner menu with prices ranging from $8 to $14. Whether you're there for lunch or dinner, take a minute to read the back of the menu. It tells the story of the area as well as giving two theories about how the towns of Trust and Luck got their names.

DETAILED DIRECTIONS

MILE 0—Turn off business US 19/23 onto NC 63 west. *The road becomes two-lane at mile 4.5. In Leicester at mile 8, you'll see some beautiful old Victorian homes. Watch your speed around mile 18—that's when the road begins to snake its way up Doggett Mountain. Tight twists and turns occupy the road until you reach Trust. St. Jude's Chapel of Hope is always open at mile 27.2.*

MILE 27.4—NC 63 ends at NC 209; turn left. *You'll find the Spring Creek Cafe on the left at mile 27.5. The "Bridge of Madison County" sits on the left side of the road, just past the cafe. You'll get a little Luck at mile 28.9. The town of Luck is just a speck, so don't blink. You'll continue through some tight twisties before the road ends.*

MILE 37.6—Turn left at the apparent end of the road to continue on NC 209. *Ferguson Supply is on the right side of the road at this intersection. This supply store has everything from gas to food to fishing supplies. You'll roll through what looks like the Scottish Highlands as you near I-40.*

MILE 46—The ride ends at the intersection of NC 209 and I-40. *Take I-40 east to head toward Asheville or continue straight on NC 209 to intersect US 74 near Waynesville.*

Trust & Luck

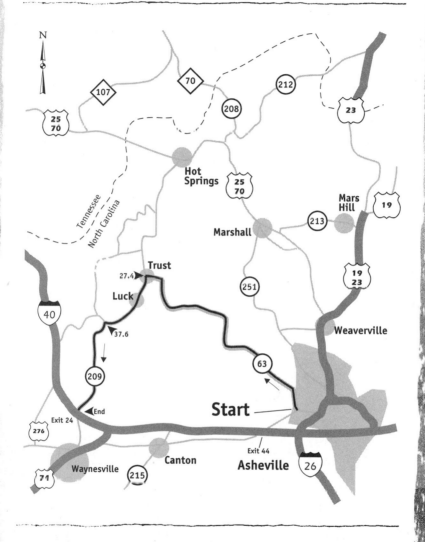

N

107
70
212
25
70
208
23

Hot Springs
25
70

Mars Hill
213
19

Marshall

Tennessee
North Carolina

Trust
27.4
Luck
251
19
23

40
37.6

209
63
Weaverville

End
Start

Exit 24
276

Canton
Exit 44
Waynesville
215
Asheville
26

71

75 Interstate Highway	28 NC State Highway	▬▬ Route
27 US Highway	91 TN, VA, SC State Highway	— Other Road
	5▶ Milepost	═══ Blue Ridge Parkway

Climbing Mount Mitchell

Ever wondered what the views are like on the highest peak east of the Mississippi? Don't like to hike? This ride is for you! Soaring to a dizzying 6,684 ft. above sea level, Mt. Mitchell invites you to ride to its peak and take in the view. On the way, you'll ride the Blue Ridge Parkway through Craggy Gardens and past Glassmine Falls. Food? You want food, too? Not to worry. Near the summit of Mt. Mitchell sits the finest restaurant for miles around.

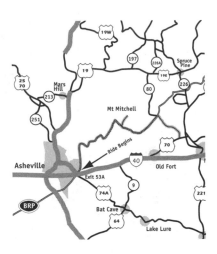

GAS

You won't spend a dime on gas during this ride! Fill your tank before you leave Asheville; you won't see another gas station until the end of the ride, 63.5 miles later!

GETTING TO THE START

The ride begins on the Blue Ridge Parkway off US 74A in Asheville. Take exit 53A from I-40 and you'll be headed in the right direction to the Blue Ridge Parkway on US 74A. Take the ramp to the Parkway and zero your trip meter as you turn right, and begin your northbound climb to Mt. Mitchell.

RIDE OVERVIEW

This ride begins on one of the most scenic roads in the country. The Blue Ridge Parkway offers great views and decent road conditions. With dozens of scenic overlooks and several tunnels, all with gently sweeping curves, it's no wonder the Parkway is a popular motorcycle destination. You'll notice after leaving Asheville and heading north on the Blue Ridge Parkway that you begin to climb in elevation. This trend will continue until you reach the summit of Mt. Mitchell at 6,684 ft.

There are two good places to stop near the start of this ride. The first is the Blue Ridge Parkway Headquarters. It's a great place to learn about visibility, weather conditions, road conditions, and other information vital to a successful trip (pick up a free map of the Parkway there, too). The next place of interest is the Folk Art Center. The Folk Art Center provides members of the Southern Appalachian Handicraft Guild an outlet to display their crafts. Most days, you'll find an artist working in the lobby. There are restrooms and a gift shop there, too.

Continuing up the Blue Ridge Parkway, your ears may pop a few times due to the elevation changes. You'll see many scenic overlooks that don't require you to dismount your bike to take it all in. One of the nicest is at mile 20.5—the Craggy Gardens Visitor Center.

Craggy Gardens is a place on the mountain where only rhododendrons grow. Trees vacated the area before European settlers arrived. Craggy Gardens is most spectacular when the rhododendron are blooming bright pink in late May to early July. Several trails will lead you on walks through the gardens, and there is ample parking.

Just past Craggy Gardens you'll pass through another tunnel. As mentioned in the road conditions section of this chapter, keep to the right half of your lane to avoid encroaching car drivers, who tend to drift to center in a tunnel.

Your reward for surviving the adventure of navigating the tunnels is a great view of Glassmine Falls at mile

TOTAL DISTANCE
63.5 miles

TIME FRAME
3 hours from start to finish. This time frame takes into account the twisty roads and overlook stops to enjoy the Parkway views. Add an hour if you plan to eat on Mt. Mitchell.

24. Glassmine Falls cascades over 800 ft. down the side of a mountain, and on a clear day, it looks like a silver ribbon shimmering on a mountainside solely for your viewing pleasure. The best views are just ahead in Mt. Mitchell State Park.

At mile 29.9, you'll be turning off the Parkway onto NC 128 and into Mt. Mitchell State Park. If you thought you were climbing in elevation on the Blue Ridge Parkway, break out the nosebleed preventer now. NC 128 climbs all the way to the top through a series of steep twists and turns.

Mt. Mitchell soars to a height of 6,684 ft. and is home to Mt. Mitchell

Fortunately, most of the climbing you'll do to reach this sign (near the summit of Mt. Mitchell) will be on your motorcycle. Mt. Mitchell is the highest point east of the Mississippi.

You've got to get up pretty early to catch the sunrise from atop Mt. Mitchell, but no matter when you're there, if it's clear, you can see the endless blue ridges.

State Park, visited by about 500,000 people annually. In the park, you'll discover many amenities. Offering restrooms, two gift shops, a restaurant, and a museum, this state park has all you'll need—except lodging. Only tent camping is available. RVs aren't allowed to camp in the park, so often you'll spot them parked between the Blue Ridge Parkway (where they aren't allowed to camp either) and the entrance to Mt. Mitchell State Park on the steep side of NC 128. So, watch for RVs in the morning on NC 128.

The State of North Carolina purchased the land for the park in 1916. For many years, the only way you could get to the summit was via a long hiking trail. An incline railway was used for a few years to carry tourists to the superb views of the summit of the mountain. Then the road was built, the railroad was abandoned, and the park has been flooded with visitors ever since.

From the summit parking lot (elev. 6,578 ft.) you'll take a three-minute hike on an improved trail to the summit. Other improvements have been made, too.

One improvement that got a new manager in 2001 is the Mt. Mitchell State Park Restaurant, offering tasty meals at reasonable prices, with breakfast costing just $5 (eggs, bacon, coffee) and lunch running you only $7 for a sandwich and a drink. For lunch, order the "Big Butt" Sandwich—named for the Virginia ham used on it, not for the posterior size of the sandwich eater, thank you. Dinner gets a little more costly with entrees ranging from about $7 to $14. There's no beer or wine, but you'll be high enough on the elevation—you won't need the alcohol anyway. The restaurant has a small gift shop and there's a museum in the same building.

Some other improvements include the stone tower adorning the top of the mountain which replaced a rickety wooden structure that crashed to the ground like the guard shack on the classic TV comedy, "F Troop." There's the Balsam Shop next to the summit parking lot. This gift shop offers souvenirs to help you prove to other bikers that you and your bike climbed the highest peak east of the Mississippi. A new park office built in 2000 offers restrooms, information, and maps, should you decide to continue your adventure on foot.

There's so much to do while visiting Mt. Mitchell, you may find it hard to leave. But when you do, it's easy to make your way out of the park—just go down! So get your fill of Mt. Mitchell and head back down NC 128 (the only road in the park) to the Blue Ridge Parkway.

Back at the Parkway, turn left (north) to continue on the route. You'll pass a few more overlooks that offer great views of Mt. Mitchell and discover a couple more tunnels before turning off of the Blue Ridge Parkway onto NC 80 at mile 51.2.

NC 80 will not disappoint you. With lots of fun twists and turns and a few hairpins, it's a real pleasure to ride. Watch for some exposed tar in the hairpin turns, though. NC 80 follows Buck Creek down the mountain. Buck Creek flows into Lake Tahoma. There's a nice view of this lake at mile 61 near the dam. Just a couple miles past the dam is the town of Pleasant Garden.

The ride ends in Pleasant Garden at the intersection of NC 80 and US 70. To head toward Asheville, turn right

onto US 70. You may want to turn left and ride into Marion where you can pick up I-40. If you have the time and energy for another adventure, try the Little Switzerland ride (it starts at the end of this route) or the Blowing Rock ride which starts in Marion at the intersection of US 70 and US 221.

Along the Blue Ridge Parkway, hardly a mile goes by without a scenic overlook.

RIDE ALTERNATIVES

You reduce the length of this ride by about an hour by staying on the Blue Ridge Parkway, passing Mt. Mitchell, and riding to the turnoff at NC 80. The only viable excuse for doing this would be low clouds obscuring the view from Mt. Mitchell.

ROAD CONDITIONS

The surface conditions on the Blue Ridge Parkway are not as great as the views from it. The Parkway is badly in need of repaving. Hazards are well marked, but watch out for a chunk of loose asphalt here and there. On the Parkway, you'll pass through several tunnels. Stay to the right half of your lane in these tunnels; cars often cross the centerline in them. NC 80 has a few "rough edges" in several hairpin turns as you ride down from the Blue Ridge Parkway. Still, any cautious biker will have no problem.

POINTS OF INTEREST

The Blue Ridge Parkway, Folk Art Center, Craggy Gardens Visitor Center, Mt. Mitchell State Park, nearly 20 scenic overlooks.

RESTAURANTS

One restaurant really stands out on this ride. The **Mt. Mitchell State Park Restaurant** offers breakfast, lunch, and dinner. You'll be surprised at the prices, too. There's no price-gouging at this out of the way restaurant. On cold days, the coffee is piping hot and on hot days the iced tea is deliciously cool. There's a small museum and gift shop in the same building.

DETAILED DIRECTIONS

MILE 0—Head north on the Blue Ridge Parkway. *You'll pass US 70 at mile 2.1. The Folk Art Center is on the left at mile 2.8. Along the way, take in as many of the scenic overlooks as you like, but be sure to check out the Craggy Gardens Visitor Center at mile 20.5. Glassmine Falls is off to the right at mile 24.*

MILE 29.9—Turn left onto NC 128 and into Mt. Mitchell State Park. *You'll find the park office at mile 32.3 with restrooms and info. At mile 33 is the restaurant/gift shop/museum. Mile 34.6 is at the summit parking area. The elevation there is 6,578 ft. You really do owe it to yourself to take the three-minute walk to the 6,684 ft.-summit and up the tower to breathe in the scenery.*

MILE 34.6—Well, that's as far as NC 128 will take you, so head back down the mountain toward the Blue Ridge Parkway.

MILE 39.6—Turn left onto the Blue Ridge Parkway. *Remember to ride on the right half of your lane as you pass through the Twin Tunnels at mile 50.5. Again, enjoy the many scenic overlooks as you ride the Parkway.*

MILE 51.2—Turn right off the Parkway onto NC 80 south. *Watch your speed and look out for loose gravel and tar streaks in the hairpin turns. Take in a view of Lake Tahoma at mile 61.*

MILE 63.5—The ride ends in the town of Pleasant Garden at NC 80 and US 70. *Turn right onto US 70 to head toward Asheville. Make a left to head into Marion to US 221, which will lead you to I-40. If you've got more time, make a U-turn and head back up NC 80 and take in the Little Switzerland ride!*

Climbing Mount Mitchell

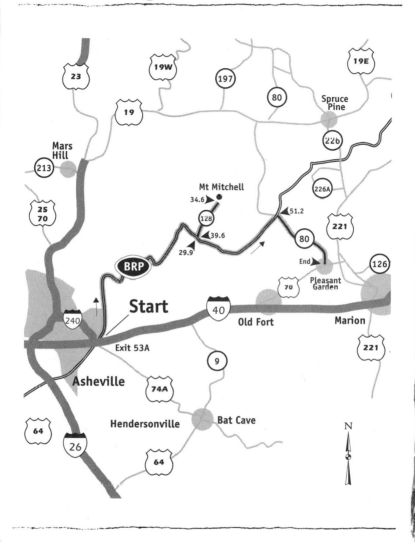

Legend:
- 75 Interstate Highway
- 27 US Highway
- 28 NC State Highway
- 91 TN, VA, SC State Highway
- 5▸ Milepost
- ▬ Route
- ▬ Other Road
- ▬ Blue Ridge Parkway

Buncombe Turnpike

This route follows the French Broad River and several creeks as you cruise part of the old Buncombe Turnpike. The turnpike leads to a wildly twisty ride into Tennessee and through the Pisgah National Forest. You won't have distant mountain views along this ride, but you will have excellent surface conditions and very little traffic.

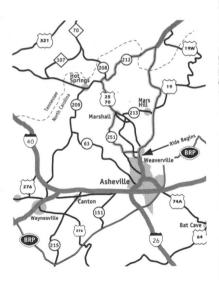

GETTING TO THE START

This ride starts just ten minutes north of Asheville from US 19. In Asheville, take I-240 to exit 4A and take US 19/23 north out of town. From US 19/23, you'll take the exit for New Stock Rd. (Weaverville). Reset your trip meter as you turn left at the bottom of the ramp to begin.

RIDE OVERVIEW

Right out of the starting chute, you'll leave the four-lane, divided US 19/23 behind, having traded it for New Stock Rd., which winds its way through a small neighborhood. You'll pass through "suburbia" pretty quickly, into rolling farm country. All this in the first four miles!

Take Monticello Rd. to the left and begin your descent to the French Broad River.

The French Broad River (actually, adding the word "river" to the name is redundant, because in this case, the word "broad" *means* river) seems to defy the laws of nature because it *flows north* through Asheville and through the mountains into Tennessee, where it meets the Tennessee River and continues down to the Gulf of Mexico. NC 251 breaks no such laws of nature as it provides you with gently sweeping curves along the banks of this great river and into the town of Marshall.

The town of Marshall rushes out to greet you in the form of a caboose on the left side of the road that serves as

GAS
Gas is available at the start and at miles 13.2, 19.4, 20, and 50.7.

an information center. Just past the caboose is the Old Train Depot. Even if it's closed when you're there, stop in and take a peek through the windows. This Depot is home to some great (and FREE!) country and bluegrass dances every Friday night starting about 7 pm. There are a few rules posted outside this depot/dance hall that are just plain funny. One rule you've probably never seen posted anywhere but here is, "No jammin' on the deck." Somewhere someone must have "jammed" inappropriately and ruined it for the rest of us. The Depot made national headlines in March of 2001 when a grandmother was escorted from the place by the local law enforcement for "dirty dancing." Look for a new rule to be posted...

Marshall is the county seat of Madison County and because of this, the courthouse and Sheriff's Office sit

TOTAL DISTANCE
52 miles

TIME FRAME
2 hours from start to finish. Include some time to get to and from this ride.

near the center of town. The side of the Sheriff's Office has a flood gauge bolted to it. How would you like that office? It floods so frequently here that the Weather Services Bureau installed a flood gauge on the side of a building—that's a sign to move your office, if you've ever heard one!

The ride takes you out of Marshall on the north side of town and joins US 25/70. On this stretch of highway you'll see some great scenery and find gas stations aplenty. Unfortunately, you'll also find lots of traffic. This short stretch of US 25/70 is a main artery for goods and services in the area. You'll just have to put up with the traffic until you meet up with NC 208 and leave the traffic behind.

NC 208 is not a turn off US 25/70. Actually, US 25/70 turns left, but you'll continue straight on, following Big Laurel Creek as it snakes its way to NC 212.

In keeping with the fine tradition of building great roads next to rivers and streams, NC 212 follows Shelton Laurel Creek beginning with gently sweeping curves through mountain country, then becomes wild with tight twists and turns as you enter Tennessee. In Tennessee, NC 212 becomes TN 352. The road number is the only substantive change to the road. The curves and excellent surface conditions continue after you cross the state line.

Marshall hangs on the edge of the French Broad River.

All too soon, TN 352 enters the tiny town of Rocky Fork, where you'll make the ride's final right turn and follow that to a left turn onto Upper Higgins Creek Rd. Upper Higgins Creek Rd. leads you from the thick woods of eastern Tennessee to the interstate-like US 19/23.

You can take US 19/23 south and be in Asheville in about an hour or head north for less than an hour to visit Johnson City.

RIDE ALTERNATIVES

You can shave off about half an hour by *not* turning left at the ride's beginning and picking up the route again on US 25/70 just north of Marshall, but why would you do that? You don't really want to miss riding next to the French Broad River, do you?

ROAD CONDITIONS

The surface conditions of this route are part of its charm. The clean, fresh asphalt on this ride is what your tires have been dreaming of. While there is a short stretch (less than ten miles) that is two-lane with commercial traffic, the rest is relatively commercial traffic-free.

POINTS OF INTEREST

The French Broad River, the town of Marshall (dance hall, etc.), Shelton Laurel Creek, and the wildlife in the Pisgah National Forest.

RESTAURANTS

The turnpike offers little in the way of food. You might want to consider packing some chow into your saddlebags before taking on this ride. There are some snacks available in the gas stations along US 70/25 and you might find a mom & pop restaurant along the roadside, but there is not much chance of finding a hearty meal along this route.

DETAILED DIRECTIONS

MILE 0—Turn left onto New Stock Rd. *(Don't be surprised that the ride cuts through a neighborhood; it was planned that way).*

MILE 2.4—Turn left onto Monticello Rd.

MILE 4—Turn right onto NC 251. *You'll be riding next to the French Broad River for the next few miles.*

MILE 13.5—Left onto business 25/70 and cut through downtown Marshall. *You'll find the Old Train Depot with dances every Friday night at 7 pm. Check out the flood gauge bolted to the side of the Sheriff's Office.*

MILE 16.6—Bear left toward US 25/70.

MILE 17.5—Turn left onto US 25/70. *You'll find gas stations along this section of the ride.*

MILE 26.8—Continue straight onto NC 208 from US 25/70. *(That's Big Laurel Creek on your left).*

MILE 30.5—Turn right at the stop sign onto NC 212. You'll be following Shelton Laurel Creek. *At mile 44.8, NC 212 becomes TN 352 as you cross the state line.*

MILE 48—Turn right at the stop sign in the town of Rocky Fork.

MILE 51.2—Turn left onto Upper Higgins Creek Rd. *This road will lead you to US 19/23.*

MILE 52—The ride ends at US 19/23. *Follow this four-lane expressway back into North Carolina and on to Asheville, or take US 19/23 north toward Johnson City, TN.*

Buncombe Turnpike

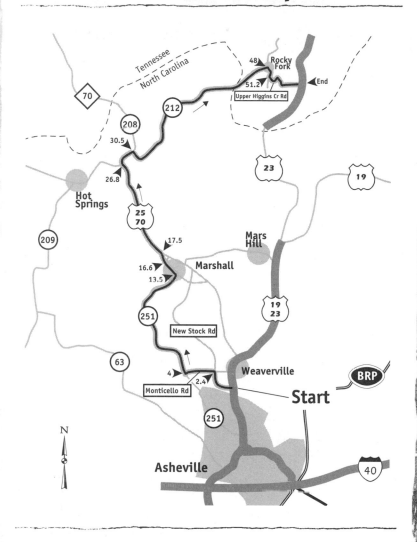

Y ou'll ride this route for the beautiful scenery of Caesars Head State Park in South Carolina. Along the way, you'll cover some great stretches of pavement. These roads have it all— tight twists, sweeping curves, and long, rolling straightaways. And the best sandwich in the universe is made along this ride, so remember to save room for a little lunch on the way.

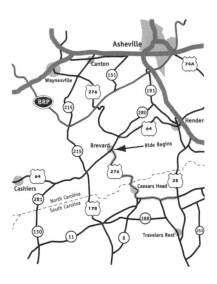

GETTING TO THE START

You'll start on US 276 south from US 64 in Brevard, NC. To get there, you can take US 64 on a long ride all the way from Tennessee into Brevard and then turn right onto US 276. From Asheville, take I-26 south, and jump off at exit 18 onto US 64 west through Hendersonville and into Brevard. Either way, zero your trip meter as you turn south on US 276 in Brevard.

RIDE OVERVIEW

As you head south on US 276 away from downtown Brevard, you'll roll in a virtual straight line most of the way to the South Carolina border. After crossing the state line, US 276 begins to climb Caesars Head Mountain in a series of tight turns and twists. The thick foliage delivers cooler temperatures, even on hot days.

Reaching the apex of Caesars Head, you'll find the State Park Visitor Center on the right side of the road. This center offers a gift shop, information center, restrooms, and a short hike to Caesars Head overlook. The overlook sits atop an 1,800-ft. vertical outcropping of natural granite, and the views from this precipice of the neighboring landscape are awe-inspiring. From Caesars Head you can see Table Rock and the Pinnacle Mountains, as well as the Blue Ridge Mountains. The trail to Devil's Kitchen begins from the overlook. Take a couple of minutes to hike this 200-yard trail through a "fat man's squeeze" crack in a rock, to get a good view of the outcropping from which Caesars Head gets its name. There are three theories as to the origin of the name Caesars Head. The true origin of the name has been permanently lost, but the theories paint a colorful portrait. The first and most popular theory is that the rock outcropping was named for Julius Caesar because it resembled the leader's profile. Another theory is that an early hunter named the place for his dog. According to legend, the hunter and his dog, Caesar, were hunting deer in the thick woods, when the dog fell from the 1,800-ft. cliff in pursuit of prey. In appreciation of his ultimate sacrifice, the hunter named the place after the dog. The third theory is that the name Caesar was the European take on the Native American word *sachem*, meaning chieftain, whose profile can be seen in the rock. Regardless of which theory you prefer, take a few minutes to investigate this area for yourself.

After filling your camera with great photos of Caesars Head, fill your stomach at the Mountain House Restaurant. You'll find this restaurant a few hundred feet past the Visitor Center down US 276. Originally a gas station and post office, this quaint stacked-stone building hides a kitchen with one of the most talented culinary staffs in the region. With tasty gourmet sandwiches for lunch, complete with a nice wine list and finished with homemade fudge and pralines, this place offers something for the most discerning palette. Dinner is also available at the Mountain House. However, it is only served on Friday and Saturday evenings from 6-8:30 pm. Lunch is served every day except Tuesdays. Dinner reservations are highly recommended. Call 864-836-7330.

US 276 continues down the southern slope of Caesars Head Mountain in a series of hairpin turns.

TOTAL DISTANCE
32.8 miles

TIME FRAME
1 hour from start to finish. Add time to walk to the Caesars Head Overlook (it's worth it) and for lunch at the Mountain House Restaurant.

In the middle of one of these turns, a small pullout on the left side of the road leads you to several acres of exposed granite. From this granite bald you can see South Carolina stretching southward toward the Atlantic Ocean. Another interesting feature of this bald is the spray paint. Apparently, if you are in love and live in the Upcountry region of South Carolina, you must bring your favorite color of spray paint to this outcropping to publicly announce your affections. Unfortunately, this bald has lost much of its appeal because of

Caesars Head looks out over the South Carolina hinterlands.

the "decorations." Still, it's a unique place to take a rest.

US 276 is joined by SC 11 and the two make a nice couple as they head northeast. Then, SC 11 diverges to the left and becomes part of the Cherokee Foothills Scenic Highway. This Scenic Highway runs straight, and you'll follow, as it takes you through a farm valley and toward US 25.

The ride ends as you turn north onto the four-lane, divided US 25 and head back into North Carolina. You'll reach I-26 in less than half an hour.

RIDE ALTERNATIVES

Sorry, there are no alternatives for this ride. Many of the nearby roads look nice on a map, but turn to dirt after a couple of miles.

ROAD CONDITIONS

US 276 is a beautiful stretch of road that offers clean asphalt with well-banked curves. Watch your speed as you negotiate through a series of hairpin turns on the south side of Caesars Head. SC 11 is part of the Cherokee Foothills Scenic Highway. You won't find any sharp twists on SC 11, only gently sweeping curves and an occasional crack in the pavement.

POINTS OF INTEREST

Caesars Head State Park with a gift shop, restrooms, an information center, and an overlook. Outside the park is the Painted Rock Overlook.

RESTAURANTS

There is only one restaurant along this ride, but it is one of the best in the area. The **Mountain House Restaurant** sits just a couple hundred yards south of the Caesars Head State Park Visitor Center. Open for lunch every day except Tuesdays, they offer

gourmet sandwiches on homemade bread. A "gourmet sandwich" includes such ingredients as grilled portabello mushrooms, seasoned turkey breast, sun-dried tomatoes, and homemade mayonnaise. To complement your meal, they offer wine and beer. Lunch will set you back about $7 for a sandwich served with chips. Top it off with a slab of homemade fudge or pralines. Dinner is served on Friday and Saturday only, from 6-8:30 pm, and will cost between $17 and $28 per entree. The dinner menu changes weekly, but the high quality remains consistent. Dinner reservations are highly recommended. You can reserve a table by calling 864-836-7330.

DETAILED DIRECTIONS

MILE 0—Turn off US 64 onto US 276 south in Brevard. *You'll enter South Carolina at mile 12.5. The road begins to get mighty exciting around mile 14. You'll find the Caesars Head State Park Visitor Center on the right at mile 15.2. The Mountain House Restaurant is on the right side of the road at mile 15.4. It looks like a remodeled 1920s gas station—because that's exactly what it is. There's a series of hairpin turns around mile 16.5. At mile 19.9, park at the small pullout on the left side of the road and walk a few feet onto a large piece of exposed granite. The locals use it as an overlook and a place to advertise their love and commitment to each other, using spray paint!*

MILE 21.8—Bear left to remain on US 276 (it's well marked). *There's a gas station at mile 27.7.*

MILE 28.2—Turn left onto SC 11, part of the Cherokee Foothills Scenic Parkway.

MILE 32.8—The ride ends where SC 11 meets US 25. *Turn right onto the access road to get to US 25, and then turn right on US 25 north to return to North Carolina and eventually to I-26.*

Hail Caesar

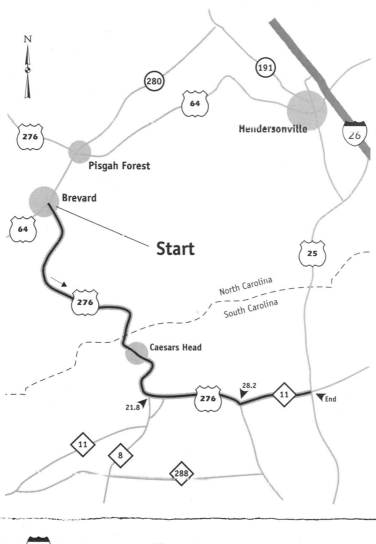

Mount Pisgah Loop

*O*ut of Asheville, over Mt. Pisgah and into the town of Waynesville is where this route takes you. Along the way, you'll take in some of the best riding the Blue Ridge Parkway has to offer, and lesser known NC 151 and US 276 as well. The Blue Ridge Parkway climbs and descends Mt. Pisgah in a series of scenic, sweeping curves, with three tunnels. NC 151 and US 276 add twisties and fun rolling hills as you make your way to and from the Parkway. There are lots of amenities, too. For great food and breathtaking views, there's the Pisgah Inn, right on the Parkway itself. Twenty minutes away, a motorcycle-only camping resort awaits. Ready to go? Let's get riding!

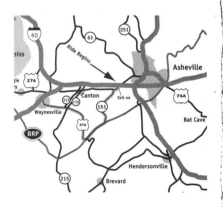

GAS

Gas is available at the start and is abundant for the first three miles on US 19/23. It's also available at miles 6.9, 18.2, 31.9, 36, 42.2, and 44.2.

GETTING TO THE START

This ride starts on US 19/23 at I-40's exit 44, just west of Asheville. After exiting I-40, turn south on US 19/23. Reset your trip meter as you turn from the exit ramp.

RIDE OVERVIEW

Soon after exiting I-40, you'll head through a highly commercialized section of US 19/23. If you are in the market for a used car or some fast food, this is your part of the ride. Watch for traffic darting out from the many businesses as you ride along this three-mile section of five-lane highway on your way to scenic and fun NC 151.

After making the turn onto NC 151 from US 19/23, you'll breathe a sigh of relief as the scenery improves. Gone are the used car lots and fast food joints. NC 151 rolls through a quiet valley in a series of wide, sweeping curves (the road was widened and repaved in 2001). Farms and country businesses dot the side of the road. As you near the edge of the valley, you'll enter a stand of pine trees, and that's where you'll begin the wild climb to the Blue Ridge Parkway.

Leaving the valley behind, NC 151 does its best to do the "twist and shout" as it takes you through some of the finest and least known hairpin turns in the region. This section is also very steep. Because NC 151 dead-ends into the Blue Ridge Parkway and no commercial traffic is allowed on the Parkway, you won't have to worry about an 18-wheeler bearing down on you as you negotiate these steep curves. For that matter, NC 151 is not a popular tourist destination, so use by vehicles of the four-wheeled persuasion is light.

Once on the Blue Ridge Parkway, you'll surely spot a car or two. Yes, the Blue Ridge Parkway is the touring vacationer's paradise. There's a good reason for this, of course; there are lots of scenic overlooks and even a couple of tunnels. In the tunnels, go ahead and enjoy the childlike fascination of honking your horn or revving your engine to hear it reverberate in the acoustically interesting conditions of these tunnels. You know you want to, and your momma won't be there to tell you not to.

Now let's turn to more grown-up pursuits, like food and a place to stay. You might be inclined to pass up the Pisgah Inn, but before you do, there

are some things about the Inn you should know. Pisgah Inn offers gas (and no, they don't gouge you; the prices are competitive with the many gas stations in the valley), food, lodging, and a gift shop.

To say that the Pisgah Inn offers "food" is a bit of an understatement. The restaurant at the Pisgah Inn offers delicious meals with spectacular views from 5,000 ft. above sea level. Dining there is a real treat. Most of the items are made from scratch. For breakfast try an omelet and coffee for about $5. For lunch, a burger and fries will set you back about $6. At dinner, try some fresh trout (read: fresh, like from trout farms at the base of the mountain) for about $13. They serve beer and wine, as well. Sorry, no beer or wine with breakfast.

Staying at the Pisgah Inn is a real treat, too. Each $75 to $87 room at this inn offers a balcony overlooking the Pisgah National Forest. The rooms here fill up fast, so make your reservations early by calling the inn at 828-235-8228, or on the web at www.pisgahinn.com.

If the Pisgah Inn's accommodations are too rich for your blood, you can enjoy the great views for just $12 nightly by camping across the street in the Pisgah Campground. Granted, you won't have your own balcony, but

Overlooks along the Parkway offer a chance for a break as well as a view.

you will be able to enjoy the views from the hiking trails in the area and from the dining room in the inn.

Farther down the Parkway you'll pass through another tunnel. If you didn't honk your horn or rev your engine before, you can do it now. If you did, you get to do it again.

About a mile past the third tunnel is the Cradle of Forestry Overlook. From this overlook you'll have a great view of Looking Glass Rock. It's the large, smooth rock face sticking out of a pine-covered mountain just to the south of this overlook. There are more views of the rock farther south on the Parkway, but they are beyond US 276 where you'll be leaving the Parkway. For more views of Looking Glass, try out the Top of the Parkway ride (p. 76).

To reach US 276, you'll turn left off the Parkway onto an access road and then turn right onto US 276. US 276 west rushes out and greets you not with a friendly handshake, but rather with a nice set of twists and turns. A few hairpin turns slice their way through the rhododendron-covered slopes.

About five miles later, you'll be nearing the town of Cruso. The welcome signs boast "Nine miles of friendly people." Many of these friendly people will be staying at the Blue Ridge Motorcycle Campground.

Nestled alongside the Pigeon River, the Blue Ridge Motorcycle Campground caters only to motorcyclists. Opened in 1984 by some motorcyclists who, after being turned away at campgrounds because they were on motorcycles, decided to beat the campground owners at their own game. They created this resort with every amenity they could afford. You'll find level campsites, a warm

This campground makes a great base for riding in the area.

bath house, a general store, a trout pond, a central campfire, and even a little restaurant (on weekends— serving breakfast, lunch, and dinner). If you didn't pack your tent, don't sweat it; they have you covered. For $38 a night you can rent a small cabin. Call ahead (828-235-8350) for the cabins—they fill up quickly. Camping is just $14 if you're alone, or $20 per couple. The grounds are beautiful. Lots of landscaping makes this resort one of the prettiest of its kind anywhere.

NC 276 begins to straighten out as you continue west toward Waynesville. You'll cross the intersection of US 276 and NC 215. By turning left there, you can start the Cradle Loop ride (p. 96). If you're hungry, try the Jukebox Junction Restaurant at this intersection for breakfast or lunch. You really do deserve a milkshake after all that hard mountain riding!

From Jukebox Junction, NC 276 remains fairly straight, but rolls over hill and dale on its way to Waynesville. In Waynesville the road seems to end. It's actually a "T" intersection with US 276 making a right turn onto Main St.

Main Street Waynesville has many shops and restaurants. The Mast General Store will be in the center of town on the left. They offer great deals on boots and other leather wear. If you're not in the market for new boots, it's still worth it to venture out in this quaint little city.

The ride ends at the intersection of US 276 and US 74. To head toward Asheville, turn right onto the entrance ramp to US 74 east. To head southwest toward Nantahala, turn left onto the southern entrance ramp for US 74 west.

RIDE ALTERNATIVES

This ride intersects the Cradle Loop ride (p. 96) as well as the Top of the Parkway (p. 76) run. Take this book with you; when you get to the intersection of the Blue Ridge Parkway and US 276, you might decide to listen to your motorcycle and do some more riding (of course, if your bike is really talking to you, do whatever it tells you to do and then seek treatment).

ROAD CONDITIONS

US 19/23 is well paved, five-lane, and dreadfully straight. Watch for cars pulling out of the many businesses along this three-mile section. NC 151 is a superb road. NC 151 has recently been widened and repaved in the valley, offering fun sweeping curves through farmland and past country businesses. It gets exciting about mile 10.5 when NC 151 begins to climb up to the Blue Ridge Parkway. NC 151 is steep, rarely traveled, well banked and in excellent shape. Watch for some gravel in the hairpin turns, though. The Blue Ridge Parkway section of this ride is in great shape. Sweeping curves abound, as does the 45 mph speed limit and the special hazard of tunnels. Stay in the right half of your lane as you pass through these tunnels to avoid cars that cross the center line. NC 276 is another excellently paved and banked road. As with many of the roads leading to the Blue Ridge Parkway, watch for some gravel in the curves.

The Parkway as it passes the Pisgah Inn offers stunning vistas.

POINTS OF INTEREST

The Pisgah Inn (gas, restaurant, lodging, camping), many overlooks on the Blue Ridge Parkway, three tunnels, Blue Ridge Motorcycle Campground.

RESTAURANTS

While fast food joints litter the side of US 19/23, do yourself a favor and hold out for something better. On Mt. Pisgah is the **Pisgah Inn**, offering breakfast, lunch, and dinner. For breakfast try an omelet for about $4, with coffee $5. Lunch will set you back $5 to $9 for burgers, fries, and a drink. Dinner of fresh trout (from the trout farms at the bottom of the mountain) run about $14. There are less expensive items on the dinner menu; prices range from $7 to $18.

    Jukebox Junction, at the intersection of US 276 and NC 215, offers a great breakfast for about $4 and lunch of burgers and fries for between $4 and $7. Not hungry? Have a milkshake!

DETAILED DIRECTIONS

MILE 0—Turn off I-40 at exit 44 and turn west (sometimes marked as south) onto US 19/23. *Watch for cars pulling out from businesses along this commercial section of the ride.*

MILE 3—Turn left onto NC 151. *You'll find a gas station there. Enjoy the freshly paved sweeping curves. The steep twisties begin at mile 10.8 as you begin your climb toward the Blue Ridge Parkway.*

MILE 15.1—NC 151 ends into the Blue Ridge Parkway; turn right. *You'll pass through two tunnels at miles 16.5 and 16.9. The Pisgah Inn (gas, lodging, restaurant, camping) is on the left at mile 18.2. Another tunnel at 19.8. 20.8*

is the Cradle of Forestry overlook, offering a great view of Looking Glass Rock.

MILE 21.6—Turn left off the Blue Ridge Parkway onto the ramp to US 276.

MILE 21.7—Turn right onto US 276. *Enjoy the many tight twists and turns as US 276 brings you down from the Blue Ridge Parkway. You'll see the Blue Ridge Motorcycle Campground on the right at mile 27.9. At the intersection of US 276 and NC 215 is the Jukebox Junction Restaurant.*

MILE 42.8—You have to turn right to stay on US 276. *In downtown Waynesville near mile 43, you'll find lots of cool shops and available parking. Stop in at the Mast General Store. Even if you buy nothing, it's a real treat (good deals on boots).*

MILE 43.2—Follow the signs out of downtown and bear left to stay on US 276.

MILE 44.2—The ride ends at the intersection of US 276 and US 74. *Take US 74 east to head back toward Asheville, or US 74 west to Sylva, Cherokee, Nantahala and points west.*

Mount Pisgah Loop

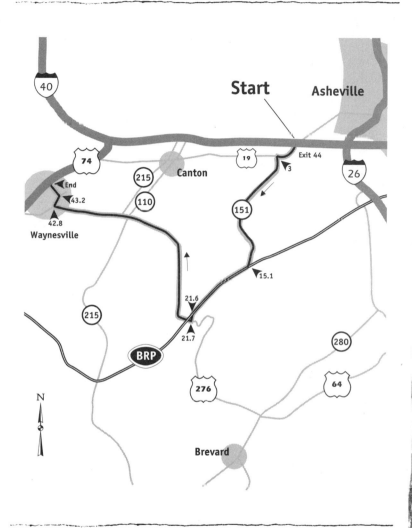

The Far West

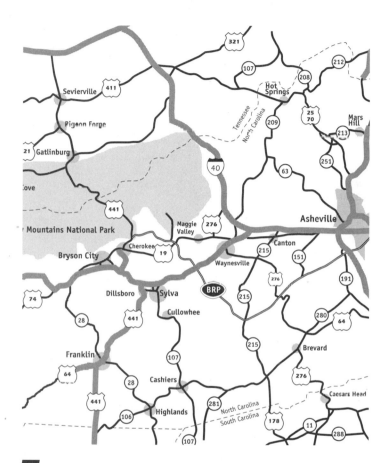

From Richland Balsam, the Blue Ridge Parkway's highest point, to the tourist town of Gatlinburg, these rides run the gamut. Whether you're touring the museum of the Cherokee Indian or climbing the observation tower at Clingmans Dome, it's an awesome mix of history, native culture, and astounding natural beauty.

Area Covered

I f hitting the "hot spots" of western North Carolina and eastern Tennessee is on your agenda, this ride is what you want. Travel from Asheville through Hot Springs, Gatlinburg, the Great Smoky Mountains National Park, and Cherokee, then round out the day with a drive through Maggie Valley. A two-lane ribbon of asphalt will twist you seamlessly from the bright lights of a tourist town into the National Park's deep wooded forest—and back. There is much to see and do on this ride, but you can elect to take in only the scenery and spectacle of it all; you are in charge.

GAS
Gas is available throughout the ride except for the 30-mile section through the Great Smoky Mountains National Park.

GETTING TO THE START

This ride starts north of Asheville where US 25/70 diverges from US 19/23. To get there, take the interstate-like US 19/23/25/70 from Asheville north about 20 miles. Near Weaverville, you'll see signs pointing the way to an exit for US 25/70; take that exit. Zero your trip meter as you turn north onto US 25/70 toward Hot Springs.

RIDE OVERVIEW

Without question, this is the longest ride in this book. It's long in distance and time, but it's equally big on adventures.

The ride starts on what appears to be a four-lane divided highway, but shortly after it begins, that highway becomes a two-lane road punctuated by sweeping curves as it rolls its way through the mountains of Western North Carolina. You'll enjoy the great road surface as you head into the town of Hot Springs.

Hot Springs gets its name from the hot springs that boil up from the earth at a temperature of 100 degrees fahrenheit. Discovered in 1778, these natural springs have a unique history. A town quickly built up around them. It was first known as Warm Springs. The name was changed to Hot Springs in 1886. During World War I, German-American citizens were imprisoned here in internment camps. Today there are no prisoners walking about, only very relaxed spa dwellers. The warm water has been channelled and now flows into modern spa tubs. The fees are relaxing, too. For just $15 per hour before 7 pm and just $25 per hour after that, it's well worth the money. If you decide to rent a spa, ask for #5 or #6 for the most privacy. The Spa offers camping ($10), cabins ($41-$128), a golf range, massage therapy, and many other amenities. You can reach the Spa at 828-622-7676.

In the town of Hot Springs just across the tracks from the Spa are two great restaurants. The Paddler's Pub and the Bridge Street Cafe compete like two banjo pickers. It seems that the best food is at one, and then the other restaurant comes up with a dish to top it. The cycle continues, creating two of the finest restaurants anywhere. Paddler's Pub has a less formal dining room and outside seating overlooking the street and a parking area. The menu includes favorites like burgers and fries as well as a complete wine and beer list, and a breakfast buffet on weekends. Plan on spending about $10 for lunch and $18 to20 for dinner. The Bridge Street Cafe (& Inn) offers dinner Thursday through Saturday, inside or on the deck overlooking Spring Creek. The Cafe's chef is from Louisiana and he can create a masterpiece from $10 to $100. From pizza to pasta and salmon to steak, this Cafe is ready to serve you just about anything you'd ever want to eat. By the way, above the Cafe is the Bridge Street Inn. The Inn is a comfortable place to crash if you've had too much wine with your dinner.

The ride begins to wind its way out of town on US 25/70 toward Tennessee. On the way, you'll find a beautiful scenic overlook of the French Broad River Valley. This

TOTAL DISTANCE
144.2 miles

TIME FRAME
5 hours from start to finish. Sure, you might be able to finish this ride in less time, but you could miss some of the coolest stuff if you rush through it. Plan to spend all day on this adventure, particularly if you are interested in the amusing attractions of Hot Springs, Gatlinburg, Cherokee, and Maggie Valley.

overlook is privately owned and the owner likes for you to register your name and comments. It's a small price to pay for such a beautiful view.

More sweeping turns await as you head into Tennessee. Once in there, the road becomes a little more narrow and twists more than it sweeps. The road crosses the French Broad River a couple of times. At one of these crossings, you'll pass over the Major Huff Bridge. This bridge is the kind with the steel superstructure. It's quite a sight—a handsome bridge.

One of the first businesses you'll come to in Tennessee is the Slab Cafe. Named for the slabs of the sawmill it was built from, the Slab Cafe offers meals seven days a week between 7 am and 9:30 pm. Gas, groceries, and video rental are available at the Slab. (Not that you'll want to rent a video for the ride, but it's nice to know you could get one if you did!)

You'll cross a set of railroad tracks and turn left onto TN 73. This freshly paved and well-banked little road is a pleasure to ride. It was built on the curvy banks of the Pigeon River. The river quietly flows southward. There's a large granite wall on the far side of the river. You can take advantage of a small gravel pullout to observe the granite wall, cool off in the Pigeon River, or eat lunch on the side of the road.

TN 73 passes under I-40 and then makes a right turn onto US 321 south. You'll start seeing signs for Gatlinburg. US 321 is a two-lane asphalt highway full of long straightaways and sweeping curves, but it has no tight twists. If you like tight twists, you'll have to wait until you enter the Great Smoky Mountains National Park. Anyway, the road leading to Gatlinburg is not extra scenic, but it does offer plenty of gas stations.

After passing the "Welcome to Gatlinburg" sign, you'll ride another couple of miles to reach the heart of the downtown business district.

On this ride you'll bisect the Great Smoky Mountains National Park.

Gatlinburg seems to redefine the term "business district." Because the businesses are so tightly compacted in this burg, you might have the sensation of riding through a shopping mall rather than a small town. Watch for pedestrians; they have the right-of-way in the crosswalks. Traffic gets so thick in the downtown area, the Gatlinburg Police Department frequently deploys officers on bicycles! The City of Gatlinburg was thoughtful enough to create plenty of parking downtown; signs pointing the way are at nearly every block. It's a small town; park and set out on foot to explore this area.

Gatlinburg is a great place for amusements. It is home to Ripley's Believe It Or Not Museum, and others too numerous to mention. There are hundreds of places to eat. The Alamo Restaurant and Saloon offers Tex-Mex food for lunch and dinner. The Alamo is located on US 321 just before the super-thick business district. The Hard Rock Cafe is in the heart of the business district at the intersection of US 321 and US 441. This place is famous for its tasty burgers and eclectic rock and roll atmosphere, and a T-shirt from the Hard Rock is a must for collectors. There are several sandwich shops as well as Belgian waffles and "carnival food" on either side of the road. Get your fill of it now, because there's little in the way of food in the Great Smoky Mountains National Park.

Unlike the gradual introduction to the Gatlinburg business district you experienced on US 321, US 441 leaves Gatlinburg and enters the Great Smoky Mountains National Park with such a sharp contrast, it is as if the business "hose" was suddenly turned off. In strong contrast to tall buildings sporting flashing neon lights, the Park's cool, lush green forests hang over the road like a tunnel. The change occurs so suddenly, it'll be a bit of a shock to your rider's brain.

According to the brochure you can pick up at the Sugarlands Visitor Information Center near the Park's northern entrance (Gatlinburg), the Great Smoky Mountains National Park is the most visited National Park in the nation. Because of this, you might want to plan your ride for a weekday when the Park is less crowded. Still, even on weekends, traffic flows without much interruption. The Sugarlands Visitor Information Center offers restrooms, vending machines, and info about the plants and animals of the Park.

As you continue on toward Newfound Gap, US 441 twists and turns so wildly that it actually twists under itself and passes through two tunnels. At Newfound Gap, you'll cross the North Carolina state line and be able to take in the view from a large scenic overlook. There are restrooms there, too. The overlook's many informational tablets describe the mountains' history and diversity, and the impact humans have made in the last couple of hundred years. Take a minute to stretch your legs and you might learn something along the way.

Just past Newfound Gap is the road to Clingmans Dome. It leads to one of the highest peaks east of the Mississippi (Mt. Mitchell is first at 6,684 ft., then Mt. Craig at 6,647 ft. Clingmans Dome rounds up the third place at 6,643 ft.). The road to the Dome is seven miles long, and then you must walk up a half mile asphalt trail (it's worth the hike) to reach the observation platform. The platform is an interesting structure, resembling a flying saucer, no doubt indicating who really designed it.

At Oconoluftee you'll see pioneers at work.

As US 441 leads you down from Newfound Gap and into North Carolina, you'll ride along a streambed and enjoy the sweeping curves the smooth road provides. There are several scenic overlooks along the way, so plan an extra few minutes to enjoy them.

Soon after the road stops descending, you'll find the Oconaluftee Visitor Center. This visitor center has restrooms, information, a working pioneer homestead and farm, and is free to visit. In the Pioneer Homestead, people dressed in the manner of the early settlers spend time teaching passing visitors what life was like in the late 1700s. For an extra measure of fun, visit the pig pen on this farm.

US 441 passes the southern end of the Blue Ridge Parkway. You'll follow US 441 out of the Park and into the town of Cherokee, on the Cherokee Indian Reservation. On the reservation, you'll find amazingly diverse attractions—moccasin and rubber tomahawk shops, a large casino, and the Museum of the Cherokee Indian, which chronicles the history and struggles of the Cherokee people. In the museum, you'll learn about the 85-character alphabet and the 1838 Trail of Tears, hear the Cherokee language spoken, and much more. Admission is just $6 for adults and $4 for kids. On hot summer days, the air conditioning alone is worth the six bucks and the things you'll learn are an extra bonus!

You'll turn left onto US 19 and follow that through Cherokee. Harrah's Casino, where you can try your luck at video gambling and slot machines, is easy to see from the road. There are no card dealers in Cherokee, but the video card dealers are nearly as fun.

US 19 begins to meander out of the downtown area of Cherokee. As you ride, you'll spot the Santa's Land Theme Park and Zoo on the left side of US 19. This is a favorite among kids of all ages and carries a Christmas theme all summer long. If you want to take in a roller-coaster ride or visit a brown bear, stop there.

You'll know you're riding out of the reservation when US 19 starts to get very twisty and sharply steep. This section is quite exciting and lacks heavy traffic. Most drivers prefer the four-lane divided US 74 that parallels US 19 north. After negotiating a mountain pass you'll descend into Maggie Valley, which is a tourist paradise. If you didn't get your fill of carnival food in Gatlinburg or Cherokee, Maggie Valley should do the trick.

Of the many attractions in Maggie, one of the most popular is Ghost Town

Sequoyah stands as a sentinal outside the Cherokee Indian Museum.

in the Sky. Open May through October, this western theme park sits atop Ghost Mountain. Getting there is half the fun. You'll buy your ticket ($20.95 for adults, $13.95 for kids) at the base of the mountain and ride a ski lift, an incline railway, or a shuttle bus (the choice is yours) to the top. Once on top, you'll be welcomed by cowboys and ladies dressed in attire from the Wild West of the 1870s. There are gunfights daily. The stuntmen who perform for you will amaze you with falls and action shoot-outs. There are several shows daily as well as saloon dances and country music performances, and twenty amusement rides to choose from.

Back in the valley, you'll find many restaurants. The most unusual is the "Salty Dog" on the right side of the road, offering tasty lunches and dinners. What is so unusual about this restaurant is how they serve their food. Don't panic when your lunch is served to you in a dog food bowl; you'll also be given a knife and fork.

Maggie Valley is also home to the Stompin' Grounds, the world headquarters for clogging. Clogging is the Southern Appalachians' most famous folk folk dance style, and is still commonly taught and performed. If you have time, check the door for the show schedule and hang out for some impressive dancing.

You'll ride out of Maggie Valley on US 19. The road will be nearly straight and is quite wide at this point of the adventure. Just when you think it's over, you'll spot Lake Junaluska on the left. This large lake is bordereded by beautiful homes and a golf course.

The ride ends where US 19 merges with US 74. You can continue straight to reach I-40, or take the next exit to reach the westbound lanes of US 74.

RIDE ALTERNATIVES

If you want to take a more direct route to Gatlinburg than the one offered on this ride, shave off the first 57 miles by beginning it from I-40 and TN 73 (that's exit 11 in Tennessee). In doing so, you'll miss some beautiful scenery, but you'll reach the tourist areas much faster.

ROAD CONDITIONS

Other than a few miles of four-lane highway at the ride's beginning and end, this ride is dominated by two-lane ribbons of pavement—mostly fresh, clean asphalt with appropriate signage. The great exception to this is the section of US 441 that runs through the Great Smoky Mountains National Park. The Park's popularity has had a devastating effect on the road condition. With cracks, potholes,

and rough spots, this scenic road is in need of repaving. There are two tunnels in the Park. Ride in the right half of your lane as you enter these tunnels. Drivers of cars tend to ride the centerline, creating head-on collision potential.

POINTS OF INTEREST

The hot springs of Hot Springs, the scenic overlook near Hot Springs, the sights and sounds of Gatlinburg (including an aquarium, Ober Gatlinburg Ski Resort, Ripley's Believe it or Not Museum and hundreds of shops), the Great Smoky Mountains National Park, the history and splendor of Cherokee (the Museum of the Cherokee Indian, many shops, and Harrah's Casino), Maggie Valley's amusements and shops (like the Ghost Town amusement park and lots of other attractions).

RESTAURANTS

There are hundreds of choices you can make during this adventure. It's all about what you're in the mood for. In Hot Springs near the start of the ride you can choose between the **Paddler's Pub** (burgers) and the **Bridge Street Cafe** (steaks and seafood). In Gatlinburg, you might want to dine at the famous **Hard Rock Cafe**, or **Alamo Restaurant and Saloon**, or one of the many other places. Perhaps, you'll choose to get a sandwich to go in Gatlinburg and picnic in the Great Smoky Mountains National Park away from the glitz and glitter. In Cherokee, there's everything from **Chinese** to **Mexican** food—it's all about choices. Maggie Valley offers some great spots, too. A favorite place to eat in Maggie Valley is the **Salty Dog** (mile 137), where your burger and fries are served in a dog food bowl. You'll spend just $9 for a burger, fries, and a beer at the Salty Dog.

DETAILED DIRECTIONS

MILE 0—Exit onto US 25/70 from US 19/23 north of Asheville. Turn left at the top of the exit ramp. *US 25/70 becomes a two-lane road at mile 8.4.*

MILE 21.2—Turn left to stay on US 25/70. *You'll enter Hot Springs at mile 26. The Hot Springs Spa is on the right at mile 26.2. Just across the tracks at mile 26.3 are the Paddler's Pub and Bridge Street Cafe.*

MILE 26.6—Turn right to stay on US 25/70. *There's a really nice privately owned scenic overlook at mile 27.5. Stop in and sign the register. You'll enter Tennessee at mile 32.5. US 25/70 becomes a little more twisty and narrow after crossing the state line. You'll cross the French Broad River at mile 35.7. The Slab Cafe at mile 42.3 offers a game room, gas, grocery, and grub. At mile 46.7, you'll cross the French Broad River again, but this time on the Major Huff Bridge. Watch for the railroad tracks at mile 50.5.*

MILE 50.5—Turn left onto TN 73 as soon as you cross the railroad tracks. *There's a nice rock wall overlooking the Pigeon River at mile 51.6 (gravel pullout, too!). You'll meet I-40 at mile 57.3; continue straight on TN 73.*

MILE 57.4—Turn right onto US 321 south.

MILE 66.5—Follow the signs and turn right to stay on US 321 south. *You'll discover a few sweeping turns around mile 76. The city of Gatlinburg greets you at mile 79.4. At mile 83.8 is the Alamo Restaurant and Saloon.*

MILE 84.7—Turn left onto US 441 south. *Watch for pedestrians! They have the right-of-way in the crosswalks. The Hard Rock Cafe is on the right after you make the left turn onto US 441. The Ober Gatlinburg Aerial Trainway is*

at mile 85.5. At mile 85.8, the shops of Gatlinburg suddenly stop and the heavy forest of the Great Smoky Mountains National Park begins. The Sugarlands Visitor Center is on the right at mile 87.4 (restrooms, vending, and info). Stay to the right side of your lane as you pass through the tunnel at mile 94.3. At mile 94.6, the road actually twists over itself. There's another tunnel at mile 99.6. You'll find the Newfound Gap Overlook at mile 100.5 as well as the North Carolina state line. To take the seven-mile side trip to see Clingmans Dome, turn right at mile 100.7. The Oconaluftee Visitor Center, complete with an old mountain farm, information, and restrooms is at mile 116.3. Mile 117 marks the southern end of the Blue Ridge Parkway. A left turn here will lead you on a 469-mile expedition to Waynesboro, VA. You'll exit the Park at mile 117.7 and enter the Cherokee Indian Reservation. The Museum of the Cherokee Indian is on the right at mile 119.2.

MILE 119.8—Turn left at the "T" intersection onto US 19. *At mile 120.9, you can meet Lady Luck at Harrah's Casino. The Santa's Land Theme Park & Zoo is at mile 123.4. Watch your speed around mile 125.4 where US 19 becomes twisty. The Cherokee Indian Reservation ends at mile 131.5. You'll pass the Blue Ridge Parkway again at mile 131.9. The city of Maggie Valley welcomes you at mile 135.6. Check out the tourist attractions in Maggie Valley including the Ghost Town, the world clogging headquarters at the Stompin' Grounds, and the Salty Dog Restaurant, where you'll be fed in dog food bowls. The shortcut to Waynesville (and many rides in this guide) is a right turn onto US 276 at mile 142.8. You'll pass Lake Junaluska on the left at mile 143.6.*

MILE 144.2—The ride ends where US 19 meets US 74.

Tourist Tour

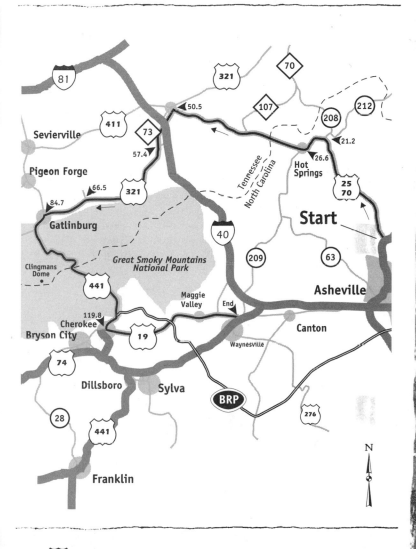

81

321

70

50.5

321

107

212

411

73

208

Sevierville

57.4

21.2

26.6

Pigeon Forge

Hot
Springs

66.5

25
70

84.7

321

Start

Gatlinburg

40

Tennessee
North Carolina

Clingmans
Dome

Great Smoky Mountains
National Park

209

63

441

Asheville

Maggie
Valley

End

119.8

Cherokee

19

Canton

Bryson City

Waynesville

74

Dillsboro

Sylva

BRP

28

276

441

N

Franklin

75 Interstate Highway	28 NC State Highway	Route
27 US Highway	91 TN, VA, SC State Highway	Other Road
	5 Milepost	Blue Ridge Parkway

*T*his route gets its name from the Richland Balsam Overlook, the highest point on the Parkway at 6,053 ft., where the views are spectacular. Along the way there, visit the Devil's Courthouse, a mountain crag from which you can see into Georgia, Tennessee, and South Carolina. The Blue Ridge Parkway is famous for its long, sweeping curves. For twisties, US 276 climbs Mt. Pisgah in a four-mile series of turns that will put a big, fat grin on the face of the most seasoned sportbiker. So, no matter what kind of rider you are, or what kind of bike you have, this ride is for you. Enjoy!

GAS

Gas is available at the start in Waynesville and at miles 1.4, 2, 7.2, 8.2, and 12.3, and then not until you exit the Parkway.

GETTING TO THE START

The ride starts on US 276 southbound in Waynesville, off US 74 exit 102A. To get there from Asheville, take I-40 west to exit 27, heading west on US 74 toward Waynesville. From the south, take US 441 north to Sylva where you'll pick up US 74 east, follow that to exit 102A in Waynesville, and turn south on US 276. Yet another way to get to the starting point is to follow US 74 east from Tennessee into Murphy, through the Nantahala Gorge, and then to exit 102A into Waynesville. Regardless of how you get there, zero your trip meter as you turn south on US 276 from US 74.

RIDE OVERVIEW

Beginning in the town of Waynesville, this adventure seems doomed to be full of traffic and shopping. While the ride ahead is much more fun than a ride through the business district, you may want to stop in a few shops to get a feel for Waynesville. One of the most colorful is the Mast General Store. They claim to have everything you need, from cribs to caskets. There are many other shops to visit, so plan a few minutes to stop on Main St. and check out the local stores.

Leaving Waynesville, US 276 becomes a straight rolling ride through the foothills of Mt. Pisgah. Along the way you'll pass farmland, new neighborhoods (which used to be farmland), and even a country club (also originally farmland). At the intersection of US 276 and NC 215 you'll find Juke Box Junction. The Junction is open from 11 am to 8 pm and offers tasty burgers, fries, and milkshakes. If you're hungry, you'd better eat now, because there is only one place to get food farther along in this adventure.

After passing through Jukebox Junction, you'll ride through the town of Cruso. The welcome sign used to read, "Cruso—9 miles of friendy people plus one old crab." I suppose the "crab" won out because now the reference to the crab has been removed from the sign. You won't find any crabs at the Blue Ridge Motorcycle Campground.

The Blue Ridge Motorcycle Campground sits on the other side of a small wooden bridge over the Pigeon

The one old crab was so crabby about this sign that the reference to him was removed.

TOTAL DISTANCE
55.5 miles

TIME FRAME
2 hours from start to finish. Add time to visit the Blue Ridge Motorcycle Campground, stop to enjoy the many overlooks along the Parkway, or hike to the Devil's Courthouse.

River. The campground was opened in 1984 to provide motorcyclists with a friendly place to camp, hang out, eat, and tell good road lies in the company of other bikers. In addition to campsites, it offers comfortable accommodations, in the form of cabins, to those who like to camp without a tent. There's plenty of hot water in the bath house and usually tons of food served up at Dee's Kitchen in the pavilion. At night, the owners build a large fire, around which the bikers gather to see who can come up with the wildest road lie. This is the kind of place where you can meet motorcyclists from all over and learn about great rides in other places. Camping is just $14 per person or $20 per couple. The cabins are $38 (single or double) a night and come complete with sheets, blankets, pillows, and even your own front porch from which to watch the festivities!

After passing the Blue Ridge Motorcycle Campground, the road gets more and more twisty as you climb up the back of Mt. Pisgah. For the next few miles the road is dominated by tight turns and steep inclines. At the top of the mountain is the Blue Ridge Parkway. This route makes a left onto the access road to the Parkway and then another left onto the Parkway, headed south. You might want to

Motorists have a tendency to ride the center line in tunnels, so stay well to the right in your lane.

If the Parkway is anything, it is well marked with signs and mileposts.

continue straight under the Parkway for a few miles to visit the Cradle of Forestry Discovery Center. This museum is an educational gem for kids and adults alike. With a cost of $4 for adults and $2 for kids, the museum is a gold mine of forestry conservation information and shows how logging methods have improved over the years. You can even try your hand at flying a helicopter simulator.

Back to our ride on the Blue Ridge Parkway, you'll find several scenic overlooks as well as picnic areas. One of the most interesting sights on the roadside is Looking Glass Rock off to the east. This small mountain is partially covered with trees, but its most recognizable feature is its smooth rocky face. When these faces are covered with ice or water, they reflect the sunlight like a mirror. The best place for viewing Looking Glass Rock is the Log Hollow Overlook at mile 27.1. There's another overlook at mile 28 that also affords a nice view.

A few miles past Looking Glass Rock is Graveyard Fields. Watch for heavy tourist traffic. No, these aren't ancient burial grounds. This area got its macabre name after a storm swept through, knocking down most of the trees. After the trees fell, their root systems looked like small burial mounds, hence the name. Today, there is no evidence of the storm, or the downed trees that created this beautiful and popular hiking spot. What you see today are lots of cars pulling into and out of the Graveyard Fields Overlook. In fact, the fields are so popular, the parking area fills early and many folks are forced to park on the side of the road.

The Parkway continues southward in a series of sweeping curves that allow you to take in the scenery. You'll pass through the Devil's Courthouse tunnel. Tunnels are an interesting and uncommon road phenomenon and are built with less frequency each year. The cost and time required to build a tunnel compared with buying extra property and grading it down to road level mean that grading has become the more cost-effective construction method. It's too bad, really, because tunnels are a cool place on a hot day, a dry place during rain, and a loud place when you rev your engine or honk your horn. Go ahead, rev that engine or honk that horn—nobody will know.

There's a dangerous thing that happens in the tunnels on the Blue Ridge Parkway. For a reason known only to the automobile gods, drivers of cars and RVs tend to creep over the center line in the path of oncoming vehicles. The prevention for this recipe for disaster is simple—keep to the right half of your lane as you enter the tunnel. That way, the car or

Bring a jacket—it's cool at 6053 ft.

RV will not hit you even if they do take over the center line.

Beyond the Devils' Courthouse tunnel, you can visit the Devil's Courthouse. Native Americans believed that the devil himself held court in a cave on this mountainside. While court has not been in session here in hundreds of years and the Park Service doesn't give directions to the cave, there is a paved trail to a beautiful scenic overlook. The hike to the overlook takes 10 to 15 minutes. Once at the overlook, you'll discover brass plaques directing you to views of mountains in Georgia, South Carolina, and Tennessee. From this overlook, you can also see the passersby admiring your bike in the parking lot.

Just a few more miles down the Parkway is the Richland Balsam Overlook. With an elevation of 6,053 ft., this overlook is the highest point on the Blue Ridge Parkway. Snapping a photo of you, the love of your life (person or bike), and the sign is a must for your scrapbook. With bragging rights secure, you can continue southbound on the Parkway.

Rolling southbound, you'll enjoy several views of Waynesville off to the right . As you near the end of this adventure, you have a couple of choices to consider. At the end of the access road from the Parkway to US 74, you can choose to turn left and head back toward Waynesville and I-40, or turn right and head toward Sylva, Bryson City, Murphy, and eventually into Tennessee. Another option is to stay on the Parkway and ride its sweeping curves all the way to US 441 in the Great Smoky Mountains National Park. Once in the Park, you can turn left and head into Cherokee to try your luck at a casino, or visit the Museum of the Cherokee Indian. Or, you may want to turn right at the end of the Parkway and ride through the Great Smoky Mountains National Park and take in the Smokin' Dragon ride (p. 84).

Whatever you decide to do, the mountain roads of North Carolina lie waiting.

RIDE ALTERNATIVES

From US 276 and the Blue Ridge Parkway, you may choose to continue straight on US 276 for a couple more miles to get to the Cradle of Forestry Discovery Center. This museum costs just $4 and will educate you about the forestry techniques used in the area.

Another alternative is near the end of the ride, where you might want to stay on the Blue Ridge Parkway and follow it all the way into the Great Smoky Mountains National Park. From there, you can turn right onto US 441 and take in most of the Smokin' Dragon ride (p. 84).

ROAD CONDITIONS

While not nearly as well known as the Blue Ridge Parkway, US 276 offers great twists and turns as you tear up Mt. Pisgah. There are plenty of signs to warn you of most hazards. Still, watch for the occasional piece of loose gravel. The asphalt on this part of the Blue Ridge Parkway is in good

When fog rolls in on the Blue Ridge Parkway, you ride in the clouds.

Take a break at the Devil's Courthouse and see if you can spot the peregrine falcons that call it home.

shape (very few cracks, little exposed tar, and no potholes). The Parkway is excellently banked and marked. You won't find sharp twists or wild bends, either—it is dominated by beautiful, sweeping curves. There is one hazard unique to the Blue Ridge Parkway, and that is tunnels—this route includes a couple or them. So, what's the problem? The problem is that car and RV drivers tend to drive over the center line in tunnels, forcing you to choose between a head-on collision with a vehicle and moving to the right half of your lane as you ride through the tunnel. So be wise and take the right half of your lane as you enter a tunnel.

POINTS OF INTEREST

The town of Waynesville (Main Street, Mast General Store), The Blue Ridge Motorcycle Campground, the Blue Ridge Parkway overlooks, tunnels and short hikes, Devil's Courthouse, Richland Balsam Overlook (elev. 6,053 ft.—the highest on the Parkway).

RESTAURANTS

There are several **fast food** joints in Waynesville, and several grocery stores. One idea is to stop in at a local grocery store, load up on goodies, and dine on the Blue Ridge Parkway. You're allowed to do this on the Parkway. Just don't forget to take your trash with you.

At mile 7.8 is the **Jukebox Junction Restaurant**, offering burgers and fries as well as great thick shakes. You'll know you're at Jukebox Junction when you see the sign shaped like a jukebox in the parking lot next to the road. Plan to spend about $8 for a burger, fries and a shake.

At the Blue Ridge Motorcycle Campground you may find Dee's Kitchen open in the pavilion. Dee prepares an excellent breakfast and single-entree dinner. If the kitchen is closed, the campground has a little shop where you can buy a bag of chips to enjoy on the road ahead.

DETAILED DIRECTIONS

MILE 0—Turn off US 74 in Waynesville onto US 276 south. *You'll find a lot of gas stations in Waynesville. It's a good idea to gas up here because gas becomes more scarce and expensive as the ride progresses.*

MILE 1—Bear right to remain on US 276 (it's pretty well marked). *At mile 1.2, you'll see the Mast General Store in the heart of downtown Waynesville.*

MILE 1.4—Turn left to remain on US 276 south (there's gas at this intersection). *Jukebox Junction Restaurant is at mile 7.8. You'll see the sign for the Blue Ridge Motorcycle Camping Resort on the left side of the road at mile 16.3. Take the wooden bridge over the Pigeon River to get there. US 276 gets mighty twisty as you begin your ascent up Mt. Pisgah at mile 19.*

MILE 22.5—Turn left onto the access road to the Blue Ridge Parkway, then turn left onto the Parkway southbound at the end of the access road. *At mile 27.1 you'll find the Log Hollow Overlook, offering the best view of Looking Glass Rock. If the rock is wet and/or icy, its mirror-like appearance shows how it got its name. If you missed the Log Hollow Overlook, there's another pretty good view of Looking Glass Rock at mile 28. Watch for traffic congestion around mile 29.9 at the Graveyard Fields; this area is popular among campers and dayhikers. As you near Devil's Courthouse, you'll pass through the Devil's Courthouse tunnel. Remember to stay in the right half of your lane through the tunnel. At mile 33.5, take a ten-minute hike up to Devil's Courthouse to see views into Georgia, South Carolina, and Tennessee. At 6,053 ft. above sea level, the sign at*

the Richland Balsam Overlook at mile 42.6 beckons you to take a photo to secure your bragging rights in your motorcycle adventure scrapbook. There's another tunnel at mile 51; stay to the right.

MILE 55—Turn right off the Parkway. *Or don't, if you want to do some more riding; follow the Parkway all the way to the Great Smoky Mountains National Park about 30 miles farther along. From there, you can turn right and take in the Smokin' Dragon ride, or turn left and visit the Cherokee Indian Reservation.*

MILE 55.5—The ride ends where the Parkway access road meets US 74. *If you turn right here, you'll be heading west on US 74 toward Cherokee, Nantahala, Murphy, and eventually into Tennessee. If you turn left at the end of the access road, you'll be heading toward the town of Waynesville, I-40, and points beyond.*

Top of the Parkway

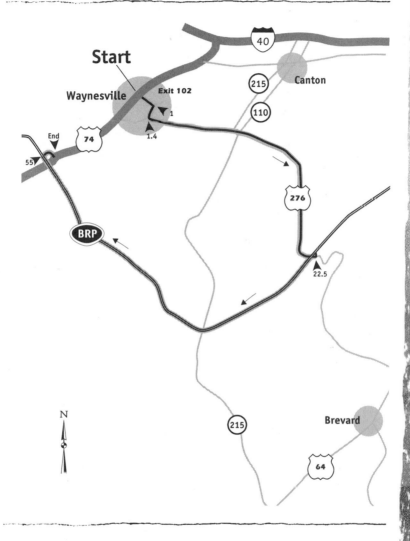

Start

Waynesville

Exit 102

Canton

40

215

110

276

End

74

55

BRP

22.5

N

215

Brevard

64

Smokin' Dragon

Smokin' Dragon takes its name from two of the finest riding destinations in the country—the Great Smoky Mountains National Park and a stretch of US 129 known simply as "the Dragon." US 441 cuts through the Great Smoky Mountains National Park, with great scenery and no commercial traffic. The Dragon is internationally famous for 318 curves in 11 miles. Civil engineers were working overtime for bikers when these two roads were made! Views and cool roads aren't the only things that make this ride great; Cherokee offers much to see and do. The 18-mile Foothills Parkway is closed to commercial traffic also, with good views of the Great Smokies to the east and the Tennessee Valley to the west.

This ride is extra long, so plan for a full day of adventure.

GAS
Gas is available at miles 0.2, 3.8, 5, 58.2, 58.6, 60, 98.4, 107.6, and 122.

GETTING TO THE START

Start at the end of the ramp from US 74 at exit 74, near Cherokee, NC. To get there from I-40, take exit 27 off I-40 and head south on US 74 to exit 74. From the south, pick up US 74 north in Murphy, NC and follow it through the Nantahala Gorge to exit 74 near Cherokee, NC. Reset your trip meter at the top of exit 74 as you turn north on US 441.

RIDE OVERVIEW

After exiting US 74 and heading north on US 441, you'll find the road is a wide four- to six-lanes. Don't worry, the route follows this highly commercial road for only the first 7.5 miles or so. As you near the downtown area of Cherokee, the road becomes two-lane and a lot more commercial. There's a well-marked left turn at mile 5.5, but going straight there will lead you to the town's many restaurants, souvenir shops, and the casino.

Before you even began this ride, you probably saw or heard the ads proclaiming Cherokee, NC to be the gambling mecca of the Southeast. While this is true, Cherokee offers much more. If Lady Luck climbed on your bike this morning and wants you to pull a few handles of the one-armed bandits, go ahead, but don't get confused by the neon and bright lights. Cherokee, NC is the tribal headquarters of the Eastern Band of the Cherokee Nation. Looking past the plastic tomahawks and rubber arrowheads, you'll find windows to the past.

In 1838, the Cherokee Indians were forced from these mountains along the "Trail of Tears." The move was brutal, to say the least. A high percentage of Cherokee died along the way to Arkansas. A few Cherokee hid from the soldiers who were rounding up the tribe and forcing it to move. Without giving up too much of the story, many Cherokee returned here to rejoin the ones who had remained hidden. Check out the complete history in the Museum of the Cherokee Indian on US 441 at mile 6.2.

Like a fire hose being suddenly shut off, the commercialism of Cherokee ends at the entrance to the Great Smoky Mountains National Park. Only a two-lane road, free of commercial traffic, lies ahead.

Two things you should focus on in the name of this Park; *Great* and *Mountains*. With beautiful and widely varying scenery, only "great" can come close to describing it. There are so many things to see and do in this Park that entire books are dedicated exclusively to it. So, here's a brief overview from a bike.

Near the Park's entrance, the Blue Ridge Parkway begins. At mile 9.2 is the Oconaluftee Visitor Center. Stop here for restrooms, maps, and to visit the farmstead museum. At mile 24.8, turn left to get to Clingmans Dome. The seven-mile ride up that road will lead you to a very unusual observation deck. It looks a little like a flying saucer, no doubt indicating who "actually" built it. The 360-degree views from the flying saucer are spectacular. You'll thank the aliens for their "advanced intelligence" design. Just past the road to Clingmans Dome is a tunnel through Newfound Gap. In

TOTAL DISTANCE
131 miles

TIME FRAME
4 hours from start to finish. Add time for stops at the Cherokee Indian Reservation, the Great Smoky Mountains National Park, and in Deals Gap.

tunnels, try to keep to the right half of your lane. Motorists tend to drive on that center line, causing many head-on crashes. At mile 31, the road gets so twisty that it actually twists under itself! Sugarlands Visitor Center marks your next left turn. This Visitor Center has vending machines, tourist information, and restrooms. After turning left at Sugarlands Visitor Center, you'll be following the Little River to your next turn at mile 55.9— onto TN 73 and out of the Park headed toward Townsend, TN.

In Townsend, although you'll find gas stations and a few places to eat, the road is less than appealing. TN 73 rolls into the four-lane US 321. Some roads are just magically under constant construction. US 321 is one of them, but you won't be on it for long. And hey, don't miss the Tuckaleechee Caverns at mile 60 (actually, you have to turn left to get to the Caverns, a short two-mile ride).

The Tuckaleechee Caverns are full of stalagmites and stalactites in huge underground rooms carved out by water over millions of years. Guided tours through the caverns lead you on a one-mile walk that lasts about an hour and costs $9 for adults and $5 for kids. Tuckaleechee Caverns is open 9 am to 6 pm seven days a week, but is closed for the season from

November 15 to March 15.

Mile 65.8 marks the ramp to the Foothills Scenic Parkway. This little-known gem of road is only 18 miles long and runs along the ridgecrest of Chilhowee Mountain. Enjoy views of the Great Smoky Mountains to the east and the cities of Maryville and Knoxville to the west. Never used by commercial traffic and rarely by others, it ends too soon at Chilhowee Lake, where you'll be making a left onto US 129 and heading into the Dragon's Lair.

As you ride next to the lake, your mind might relax a little. That's good; conserve your energy for the battle ahead. There's a dragon just round the next bend, and you must slay it! Okay, it's not a real dragon, but it's so twisty and curvy that motorcyclists from all around the country call it by that name. With 318 curves in 11 miles, it's an engineering feat! No matter what kind of bike you're riding, you're sure to enjoy it. Sportbikers like to take the curves pretty fast, so wave them around if you can. If you're the sportbiker, try to demonstrate a little restraint when it comes to dealing with other traffic. Don't give motorists a chance to create negative images of sportbikers. There are already too many bad stereotypes in motorcycling.

As you enter North Carolina from Tennessee, you'll be riding down into Deals Gap and the last curve of the Dragon. At the intersection of NC 28 and US 129 you'll spot the Deals Gap Motorcycle Resort Campground, which caters only to motorcyclists. It's open April 1 to December 1 and you'll probably also find it open on really nice winter weekends. The campground is about the size of a football field between the motel and the road. It costs just $12 nightly to set up your tent, with motel rooms

Take it easy in the Dragon's curves and you'll keep your ride looking good.

just $49 for two people in the room.

Here also you can buy your much-deserved and highly coveted "I Slayed the Dragon" T-shirt. Rob Pemble owns the Resort and used to own Sport Touring Accessories in Dillsboro. He moved all those great sport touring accessories right to where you'll need them the most, at the end of the Dragon, and he's added a little sandwich shop to this convenient storefront. If you're strapped for cash and plan to spend only a little, spend it here. Supporting motorcycle-only outposts like this one can only be good for the sport of motorcycling. And in case your bike needs some work, the Dragon Works sits next to the motel and offers tires and full service repairs.

Leaving Deals Gap, turn left onto NC 28. It skirts the north shore of Lake Cheoah as it snakes toward Fontana Dam and Fontana Village.

Fontana Dam is the highest concrete dam east of the Rockies. Consider a tour into the bowels of the dam to see the control room and giant turbines. Fontana Village was home to the workers who built the dam. A popular place to stay when Deals Gap Motorcycle Resort has no vacancy, Fontana Village is accustomed to motorcyclists and offers reasonably priced accommodations.

NC 28 continues east on the south shore of Lake Fontana. The lake is huge (11,685 acres), with over 200 miles of shoreline. You can rent a houseboat from Fontana Village and stay, literally, on the lake for an interesting perspective of the mountains (sorry, no motorcycles allowed on the houseboats).

The ride passes through another section of continual construction near the ride's end on NC 28. For some unknown reason, the traffic engineers decided to take out all the good curves and replace them with a four-lane divided highway. So be prepared for a little traffic as the ride ends.

This ride ends when NC 28 "T's" into US 74. If this long ride wasn't enough for you, try out the Franklin Loop ride (p. 100). Get to its starting point by turning left on US 74 and then right onto NC 28 at the gas station. To head back to I-40 from the ride's end, turn left onto US 74 and follow it north. To get to Murphy, NC and points south and west, turn right at the ride's end and follow US 74 through the Nantahala Gorge and beyond.

RIDE ALTERNATIVES

There's no way to shorten this ride, but there are a couple of ways you can lengthen it. At mile 24.8 you can make a left turn and ride just seven miles to Clingmans Dome. There's a really cool 360-degree observation platform just a half mile (it's worth the hike) from the parking lot at the end of the road. At mile 38 the ride makes a left to avoid Gatlinburg, TN. If you want to go to this cool town to eat, drink, and be merry, keep going straight on US 441; you'll be in the center of town in less than ten minutes. Always wanted to go to Dollywood? US 441 north will take you to Pigeon Forge, home of country music diva Dolly Parton and Dollywood.

ROAD CONDITIONS

Generally speaking, there's little in the way of commercial traffic on this ride, but US 441 gets covered with RVs late in the day. To avoid having to follow a lumbering Winnebego through the Great Smoky Mountains National Park, start the ride early— definitely before lunch. The asphalt through the Park is in desperate need of repaving, with a few potholes and some loose patches to keep you on your toes. The Foothills Parkway offers superb scenery, no traffic, and clean (but older) asphalt. US 129 (a.k.a. the "Dragon"), is a very twisty piece of road and offers fresh young asphalt with few spots of gravel. NC 28 flows from Deals Gap in a series of fun twists and turns with little patches of exposed tar to keep you on your toes. About 15 miles from the end of the ride, NC 28 becomes a four-lane divided highway. Except for loose gravel, potholes and a patch of exposed tar, hazards are well marked.

POINTS OF INTEREST

Cherokee, NC: Cherokee Indian Reservation, casinos, food, the Museum of the Cherokee Indian, shopping galore. **Great Smoky Mountains National Park:**

Oconaluftee and Sugarlands Visitor Centers, Tuckaleechee Caverns, Foothills Scenic Parkway, The "Dragon," Deals Gap Motorcycle Resort and Campground (source of the "I Slayed the Dragon" t-shirts).

RESTAURANTS

For such a long ride, this one offers very little in the way of cuisine. There's fast food galore at the ride's beginning near Cherokee, NC (and an ample supply of Belgian waffles and other "tourist" food). A few places in Townsend, TN will compete for your dining dollar. The Deals Gap Motorcycle Resort and Campground might as well add "and Sandwich Shop" to its already long name. It offers colds drinks (no beer or wine; drinking doesn't mix with dragon slaying), chips, and sandwiches for about $5.

DETAILED DIRECTIONS

MILE 0—Turn onto US 441 north from US 74, exit 74 near Cherokee, NC. *There's a water wheel and old mill at mile 3.2.*

MILE 5—Turn right to stay on US 441 north.

MILE 5.5—Turn left to stay on US 441 north. *Continue straight to head into downtown Cherokee. On this road you'll find many places to eat. Mile 6.2: Museum of the Cherokee Indian (open daily 9am to 5pm). Mile 7.8: you'll enter the Great Smoky Mountains National Park. At mile 8.3 is the start of the Blue Ridge Parkway. Mile 9.2 is the visitor center with the farmstead museum behind it (restrooms, too). Mile 24.8: Enter Tennessee. Turn left here to ride the seven miles to Clingmans Dome. At mile 25 you'll pass through the Newfound Gap tunnel. At mile 31, the road loops under itself.*

MILE 30—Turn left at Sugarlands Visitor Center. *Vending machines, restrooms, and information are here. For Gatlinburg and Dollywood, continue straight on US 441 north.*

MILE 55.9—Turn right onto TN 73 toward Townsend. *At mile 56.7 you'll leave the Park and find gas stations and food. The turn to the Tuckaleechee Caverns is at mile 60.*

MILE 65.8—Turn left onto the ramp to the Foothills Scenic Parkway, making a right turn at the bottom of the ramp.

MILE 83.2—Turn left onto US 129 at the end of the Parkway. *You'll ride next to Chilhowee Lake for a few minutes, then enter the Dragon's Lair at mile 86.4. At mile 97.7, enter North Carolina—Deals Gap is just around the next curve. At mile 98.4, stop in at Deals Gap Motorcycle Resort for a shirt to commemorate your excellent dragon-slaying adventure. When you're done celebrating, make a left turn onto NC 28.*

MILE 90.4—Turn left onto NC 28. *NC 28 follows Lake Cheoah for a few miles on its way to Fontana Village. Mile 107.6 is Fontana Village with gas and lodging. At mile 109.2, NC 28 makes a right turn (if you miss it you'll just end up visiting the Fontana Dam, which isn't a bad idea anyway).*

MILE 131—The ride ends at the intersection of NC 28 and US 74. *Turn left onto US 74 to head north toward I-40, or turn right to head south through the Nantahala Gorge toward Andrews and Murphy, NC. If you aren't pushed for time, add two hours to your riding day by trying out the Franklin Loop ride (p. 100). It starts just three minutes north on US 74 at NC 28 south.*

Smokin' Dragon

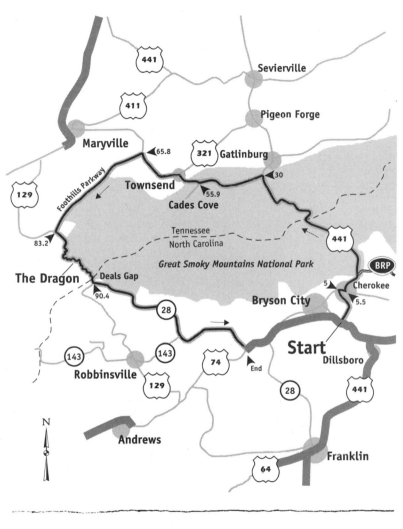

441

Sevierville

411

Pigeon Forge

441
◄65.8

321 Gatlinburg

Maryville

30

129

Foothills Parkway

Townsend

55.9

Cades Cove

Tennessee
North Carolina

441

Great Smoky Mountains National Park

BRP

83.2

The Dragon

Deals Gap

5

Cherokee

90.4

Bryson City

5.5

28

Start

143

143

Dillsboro

74

End

28

441

Robbinsville

129

Andrews

441

N

Franklin

64

Legend

75	Interstate Highway	28	NC State Highway	▬▬▬	Route
27	US Highway	91	TN, VA, SC State Highway	▬▬▬	Other Road
		5 ▶	Milepost	═══	Blue Ridge Parkway

Cullasaja Gorge Run

Superior road conditions rule on this ride. The views are spectacular, too. Care to drive under a waterfall? Here's your chance. This route takes you beneath *Bridal Veil Falls*. Along the way, you'll drive through the highest incorporated town east of the Mississippi (Highlands, at 4,118 ft.), and through the resort town of Cashiers, where the Thorpe Reservoir beckons you to stop and sit on its banks. With one gorge, two villages, three waterfalls, and a beautiful reservoir all on excellent roads, you'll find this ride difficult to pass up.

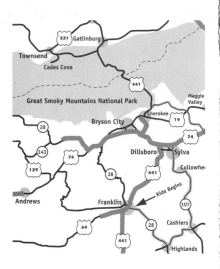

GETTING TO THE START

Start this ride on NC 28 off US 441 in Franklin, NC. From I-40, take exit 27 onto US 74 south and follow US 74 to exit 81 onto US 441 south. Follow US 441 south into Franklin and turn left onto NC 28 south, heading toward Highlands. Reset your trip meter as you turn left from US 441.

RIDE OVERVIEW

Leaving the slab of US 441 behind, you'll appreciate the comfortable sweeping turns of NC 28 as you make your way through the town of Cullasaja en route to the gorge of the same name. Use this time to warm your tires for the twisty climb to Highlands.

Soon you'll see signs warning truckers that the road is not really designed for them. It has 15 mph curves and steep uphill grades—a real beast in an 18-wheeler. These signs might as well say something like "Motorcyclists, Enjoy!" Just past the warning signs is the beginning of the climb up and through the Cullasaja Gorge.

If you've never ridden through Yosemite National Park, the Cullasaja Gorge offers a glimpse of what it's like—a tiny road carved out of the side of a cliff, opposite a large sheer rock face, and separated by a chasm so deep that you fear the road's edge. There is but one (and it is very small) pullout in the Cullasaja Gorge.

This pullout is near the Cullasaja Waterfall at mile 8. Because you've been concentrating on keeping your bike on the road and not flipping it over the small stone curb into oblivion, this pullout is likely to be your only chance to actually see the gorge. This is one of those times when a passenger has the best seat on the bike. Let your passenger have a camera and snap a few shots of the gorge as you play the part of mountain goat motorcyclist.

Leaving the gorge behind, the road widens a bit as it leads you to Dry Falls. Unlike Cullasaja Falls, Dry Falls, at mile 13.7, offers ample parking and a good path leading you on a three-minute hike to walk beneath it. You'll pay just $2 for the convenience of parking and taking in the trail. It's worth the money. Besides a break from the road, the walk to the falls will give your legs some good exercise. This waterfall got its name because a person can stand under it without getting wet. You'll probably discover that whoever came up with the name had a different definition of dry than you do.

Bridal Veil Falls will keep you dry even as you ride under it. You'll find it

TOTAL DISTANCE
56.5 miles

TIME FRAME
2 hours from start to finish. Add time for short hikes to two waterfalls, shopping in Highlands, getting food in Cashiers, and picnicking along the shore of Thorpe Reservoir.

at mile 14.7, where an old section of NC 28 cuts under the falls. You're still permitted to ride on that old section. A photo of you on your bike riding under a waterfall is a must for your "Tales from the Road" scrapbook. After leaving Bridal Veil Falls, Highlands greets you with a beautiful pond.

With an elevation of 4,118 ft, Highlands bills itself as the highest incorporated town east of the Mississippi. You'll discover not only high elevation, but high prices, too! With many small shops, this place is a shoppers' paradise. It's fun just to browse. Besides, where would you put all that stuff you buy, in your tank bag?

Signs like this might as well say, "Motorcyclists, Enjoy!"

A word about Main Street in Highlands. Whoever designed the downtown parking arrangement deserves an award of some sort. Main Street, also known as NC 28, is quite wide and cars park on both sides of the road. That's not too unusual, right? Well, in Highlands, you can park in the *middle* of Main St. This gives the passing motorcyclists an exciting obstacle course as people pull out of parking spaces from every conceivable direction—sort of like running the gauntlet. Enjoy.

Assuming you've survived the adventure of the parking gauntlet, let's eat! If you decide to dine in Highlands, be ready to drop some money on lunch. The average hamburger here will set you back about six bucks (and that's just for the burger!). If you're in the mood for the least expensive dining, try one of the many sandwich shops or the pizza place on Main St. For just a few bucks more, try the Rib Country Restaurant on NC 28 south just off of US 64. To get there, turn right onto NC 28 south where NC 28 and US 64 diverge at mile 17.4. Go one block, and it'll be on your left. For fine dining with a view, try the Skyline Lodge and Restaurant. The Skyline Lodge sits on Flat Mountain Rd. at mile 19.8. You'll ride down Flat Mountain Rd. about a mile to get to the restaurant. The views are spectacular and the prices are, too.

If you can hold out on eating until you reach Cashiers and you really like barbecue, ride just ten miles past Flat Mountain Rd. to the Carolina Smokehouse & Barbecue, which offers the best dining/dollar exchange rate in the area. You'll get an enormous barbecue sandwich, fries, and an iced tea (sweet, of course) for about $5. If you can figure out a way to pack it on your bike, get the order to go so you can enjoy it on the banks of a quiet

Dry Falls of the Cullasaja River.

mountain lake. Then turn from US 64 onto NC 107 and head toward Thorpe Reservoir.

Thorpe Reservoir is a large lake made to produce power for the region. It's also a recreational site—for fishing, boating, water skiing, and picnicking along its shore. You get the picture. At mile 31.8 there are two small gravel pullouts on the left side of the road. You can park your bike there and take a short walk over the guardrail to a beach to enjoy your lunch. There are no signs prohibiting this. To make sure none are ever posted, clean up after yourself. Better yet, if somebody else has trashed the beach, take some of that with you, too.

So, maybe you're just not satisfied with picnicking along the shore of this lake and you want to adventure out onto it. Unless you have a really impressive trailer rig on your bike, chances are you didn't bring your boat. You can rent a boat from the Signal Ridge Marina at mile 32.6. They have everything from canoes to ski boats. You can rent their large pontoon boat for eight hours for $150, plus gas. A ski boat will run you $35 an hour (two-hour minimum), plus gas. If you're thinking of renting a boat, book early; reservations fill up two weeks in advance. Call them at 828-743-2143 or visit them on the web at www.signalridgemarina.com.

After passing Thorpe Reservoir, the road continues to twist its way down a steep grade. You'll be led through a wide valley and to Western Carolina University. The campus of this fine learning institution sits on the right side of NC 107 as you continue into Sylva.

If you haven't eaten by the time you reach Sylva, consider stopping for lunch or dinner at Lulu's, a bistro-style establishment with an eclectic menu (and a great wine list!) sure to please vegetarians and carnivores alike. This place has received rave reviews from restaurant critics. Lulu's is right on Main St.

From Sylva, you'll need to turn right to reach US 74 and the end of the ride, or take the ride alternative by continuing straight on US 23 business to cut through Sylva to Dillsboro, where you can pick up US 441.

RIDE ALTERNATIVES

Near the end of the ride, you can elect to stay on US 23 business and ride through Sylva to Dillsboro, returning to US 441 in just three more miles. This alternative is particularly useful if you want to head south on US 441.

Enjoy the curves as you make your way down from Cashiers to Cullowhee.

ROAD CONDITIONS

NC 28 from Franklin into Highlands is in excellent condition. Freshly paved and well banked, it is a pleasure to ride. In the Cullasaja Gorge, watch the road. The "guardrails" are actually just one-foot-tall rock curbs. Motorcycle crash dynamics tell us that's just high enough to jettison you from your bike into the deep chasm that is the Cullasaja Gorge, so let your passenger do the sight-seeing. The brief section of US 64 from Highlands to Cashiers is in serious need of repaving. Expect a few shallow potholes and loose gravel throughout. Once you turn onto NC 107, the road becomes hospitable again, well banked and excellently paved. NC 107 invites you to ride its sweeping curves with no worries.

POINTS OF INTEREST

Cullasaja Gorge, Cullasaja Falls, Dry Falls, Bridal Veil Falls, towns of Highlands and Cashiers, Thorpe Reservoir, Western Carolina University campus.

RESTAURANTS

In Highlands it's all about how much time and money you're willing to spend. Try a **sandwich** or **pizza shop** downtown, or the **Rib Country Restaurant** on NC 28 just south of your turn onto US 64. If you prefer fine dining, try the **Skyline Lodge and Restaurant**. It sits on the side of a mountain on Flat Mountain Rd. Turn left at mile 19.8 to get there. It's expensive food, but the scenery makes it worthwhile, and reservations are recommended. For something a little cheaper, try the regionally famous **Carolina Smokehouse & Barbecue** in Cashiers. This fine barbecue restaurant sits on the side of US 64 at mile 27.5 and offers some of the best barbecue in the area. Order to go and picnic on the banks of the Thorpe Reservoir at

mile 31.8. In Sylva, try **Lulu's** on Main St. for lunch or dinner.

DETAILED DIRECTIONS

MILE 0—Turn off US 441 in Franklin and head south on NC 28 (also marked as US 64 east). *View the Cullasaja Falls and Gorge at a precarious pullout at mile 8. Mile 13.7 is where you visit Dry Falls. It's just $2 to park and walk three minutes to the falls. At mile 14.7, ride under Bridal Veil Falls. You'll enter downtown Highlands at mile 17.*

MILE 17.4—Turn left onto US 64 east. *If you want to eat at the Skyline Lodge, turn left onto Flat Mountain Rd. at mile 19.8. The Carolina Smokehouse & Barbecue Restaurant is in Cashiers at mile 27.5.*

MILE 27.7—Turn left onto NC 107. *At mile 31.8 are two small gravel pullouts next to the shore of Thorpe Reservoir. You can rent a boat from the Signal Ridge Marina at mile 32.6. See the campus of Western Carolina University at mile 47. Near mile 53, you'll enter Sylva.*

MILE 54.8—Turn right to stay on NC 107. *The ride alternative starts here. Instead of making a right, continue straight on US 23 business. If you make no turns, it will lead you through Sylva, then Dillsboro and onto US 441. Staying with the route as written will lead you out of Sylva and onto US 74 north. If you don't want to go north, don't despair, just make a U-turn at the next intersection.*

MILE 56.5—The ride ends at the jct. of US 74. *Head east to Asheville or west to Nantahala and beyond.*

Cullasaja Gorge Run

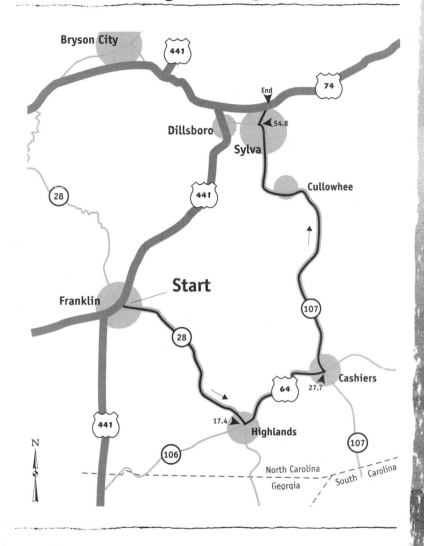

Bryson City

Dillsboro

Sylva

Cullowhee

End

54.8

Franklin

Start

28

64

27.7

Cashiers

17.4

Highlands

106

107

North Carolina

Georgia

South Carolina

N

	75	Interstate Highway		28	NC State Highway		Route
	27	US Highway		91	TN, VA, SC State Highway		Other Road
				5	Milepost		Blue Ridge Parkway

Cradle Loop

This 78-mile loop posts signs for truckers which read, "5000 ft elevations, 15 mph curves, and 9% grades along this route." Those warnings to commercial vehicle drivers might as well be an invitation to motorcyclists! This ride offers much to the visiting biker, including a motorcycle-only campground, the Cradle of Forestry Discovery Center, and superb views with little traffic.

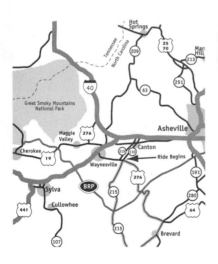

GAS
Gas is available at miles 27, 38, 40.7, 73.8, and near the ride's end at mile 78.

GETTING TO THE START

From I-40, take the exit for NC 215 in Canton, NC and follow the signs south to the intersection of NC 215 and US 276—it's a nine-mile ride off the interstate to the start of the ride. Reset your trip meter as you turn right onto NC 215 south at its intersection with US 276.

RIDE OVERVIEW

Right there at the ride's beginning, you'll find Jukebox Junction. This quaint soda shop is open Tuesday through Saturday from 11 am to 8 pm offering burgers, dogs, and sodas. The start is just across a small bridge.

Turning right onto NC 215 south, you'll see the sign warning commercial vehicle drivers of the "5000-ft. elevations, 15 mph curves, and 9% grades." A trucker's curse is a motorcyclist's fancy. Commercial traffic seldom uses NC 215.

NC 215 won't start climbing right away; enjoy rolling hills and farmland as you begin this ride. Curves begin in earnest after you pass Lake Logan.

Lake Logan is a private lake with many signs warning that trespassers will be severely dealt with. It's owned by the Episcopal Church, and you won't want to tangle with the great I AM by trespassing.

Just past the lake, NC 215 begins its twisty dance upward toward Beech Gap, following the west fork of the Pigeon River. Many waterfalls and wild rapids make the scenery spectacular.

Once you climb your way to Beech Gap, you'll cross the Blue Ridge Parkway. (To shave off more than half of this ride, you can go north on the Parkway and rejoin the route on US 276. In doing so, though, you'll miss most of the scenery along the route.) Then, settle into the rhythm of turns and twists as you make your way down this lush, rhododendron-covered road on your way to US 64 in Rosman.

In Rosman, turn left onto US 64 from NC 215. This stretch offers fast food, a few gas stations, and even a Victory Motorcycle dealership, but no fun curves or beautiful scenery. In a quick 13 miles or so, the slab of US 64 is replaced with the two-lane, twisty US 276 slicing through the Pisgah National Forest.

Turning from US 64 onto US 276, you'll leave the four-lane behind. You'll find the Hawg Wild Bar-B-Que Restaurant at this intersection, along with Dolly's Dairy Bar. If your stomach is grumbling, better eat now; there's little in the way of food in the Forest.

Within the Pisgah National Forest, superb scenery and nice road conditions await. Looking Glass Falls is within sight of the road; a five-minute walk will take you to the base of the falls. Don't miss the Cradle of Forestry Discovery Center.

As you continue your climb toward the Blue Ridge Parkway, you'll notice that a lot of the tourist traffic won't follow you. Their interest in US 276 ends at the Cradle Of Forestry. Too bad for them, too good for you!

You'll pass under the Blue Ridge Parkway and begin your descent to the end of the ride. Enjoy the curves

TOTAL DISTANCE
78.4 miles

TIME FRAME
2 hours from start to finish. Add an hour if you're riding this route in the summer, due to vacationer traffic along US 276. Schedule in an extra couple of hours for visiting the Cradle of Forestry Discovery Center, or to take a short hike to Sliding Rock.

and twists as you lose altitude. This part of US 276 is in excellent shape.

Once US 276 levels out, you know you're getting close to the Blue Ridge Motorcycle Campground. This motorcycle-only campground was opened in 1984, and now has a loyal following; it stays full from May to October. If you don't wish to camp, call ahead for a cabin. You'll actually be reserving a *bedroom* in a cabin. Don't worry that there's no kitchen; the campground usually serves breakfast and dinner. In the evening, join other motorcyclists around the campfire and share a good road lie— just remember to embellish! The Blue Ridge Motorcycle Campground can be reached by phone at 828-235-8350. Cabin rentals must be prepaid, but camping requires no reservations. It's a huge place that has never turned away a camping motorcyclist. At the very least, stop in at the gift shop and support this business so it will be here for future generations.

The ride rolls along a few miles past the campground, and ends where it began at the intersection of US 276 and NC 215. Return to civilization by continuing straight on US 276 into Waynesville, or following NC 215 north into Canton and on to I-40.

RIDE ALTERNATIVES

You can avoid all kinds of traffic—and the painful, 13-mile stretch of "slab" known on this route as US 64—by climbing to the Blue Ridge Parkway on NC 215 and taking the Parkway north to US 276. This alternative is a major compromise. You'll cut the ride in half, but you'll pay dearly by missing the Cradle of Forestry Discovery Center and many of the ride's other attractions.

ROAD CONDITIONS

As with most roads in North Carolina, you can just about count on some sand and small gravel left over from the snow-clearing process. NC 215 and US 276 are in great shape, but hazards are poorly marked. The 13-mile section of US 64 is straight and dull with lots of traffic to contend with.

POINTS OF INTEREST

Views of Lake Logan, the Blue Ridge Parkway, the roadside pullout at Looking Glass Falls, the hike to Sliding Rock, the Cradle of Forestry Discovery Center (helicopter simulator, etc.), and the Blue Ridge Motorcycle Campground.

RESTAURANTS

At the ride's beginning, you'll see the **Jukebox Junction Restaurant**. It offers lunch and early dinner Tuesday through Saturday 11 am to 8 pm. Burgers, hotdogs, and sodas are on the menu. At the entrance to Pisgah National Forest on US 276 just off US 64 is **Hawg Wild Bar-B-Que**, with delicious North Carolina barbecue for lunch and dinner. If you're looking for something a little lighter, try **Dolly's Dairy Bar** across the street from Hawg Wild. A cold ice cream is an excellent accent to an already great ride. If you can hold off your hunger until mile

69.7, try out Dee's Kitchen at the Blue Ridge Motorcycle Camping Resort. She cooks a mean breakfast and dinner, but no lunch.

DETAILED DIRECTIONS

MILE 0—Turn right onto NC 215 south. *At mile 2.9 you must turn left to remain on NC 215 south. It's well marked. You'll see Lake Logan at mile 6.8. This is a private lake and they take trespassers seriously, so enjoy the view from the road. At mile 18.2, NC 215 meets the Blue Ridge Parkway. You can start the ride alternative here by heading north on the Parkway toward US 276.*

MILE 35.5—Turn left onto US 64. *If you're looking to buy a new bike, try out the Victory dealership on the left side of the road at mile 42.9.*

MILE 48.4—Turn left onto US 276. *Just before entering Pisgah National Forest, you'll find the Hawg Wild Bar-B-Que as well as Dolly's Dairy Bar. Looking Glass Falls can be seen from the roadside pullout at mile 54. At mile 56.2 is the paved driveway to the Sliding Rock hiking area, with the Cradle of Forestry Discovery Center at mile 59.6. At mile 63.6, you'll pass under the Blue Ridge Parkway again. Find the Blue Ridge Motorcycle Camping Resort at mile 69.7.*

MILE 78.4—The ride ends at the intersection of US 276 and NC 215. *Go straight at the end to get to Waynesville or follow NC 215 north as it makes its way back to I-40 in Canton.*

Cradle Loop

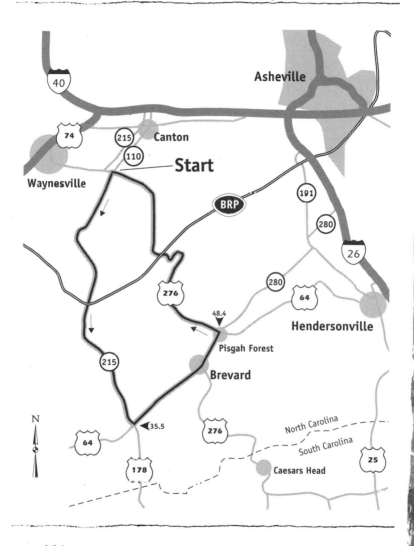

Asheville

40

74

215 Canton

110 Start

Waynesville

BRP

191

280

26

276

280

48.4

64

Hendersonville

Pisgah Forest

215

Brevard

N

35.5

64

276

North Carolina

South Carolina

25

178

Caesars Head

Symbol	Description
75	Interstate Highway
27	US Highway
28	NC State Highway
91	TN, VA, SC State Highway
5 ▶	Milepost
▬▬	Route
▬▬	Other Road
▬▬	Blue Ridge Parkway

Franklin Loop

In the first quarter mile, you'll be spun through a series of wild twists and turns that don't let up until the ride ends. Taking you from farmland to a small town to the peak of a mountain, and ending only after passing through a gorge, this route offers some of the most diverse terrain in this guidebook. With lots of great roads and little traffic, you'll return to this ride again and again.

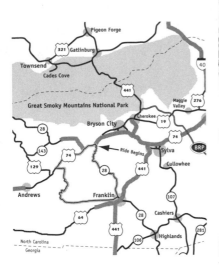

GAS
Gas is available at the start and at miles 15, 21.2, 26.1, 44.3, 63.3, and at the ride's end.

GETTING TO THE START

Begin at the intersection of US 74 and NC 28. These two roads intersect twice, so be sure to take NC 28 south from US 74. Getting there from I-40, take exit 27 south onto US 74 and follow that to the first intersection with NC 28 (near Bryson City). From the south, follow US 74 north from Murphy, NC and turn right at the second intersection with NC 28. Either way, it's the only US 74/NC 28 intersection with a Texaco. Reset your trip meter as you turn off of US 74 onto NC 28 south.

RIDE OVERVIEW

Leaving the four-lane divided US 74 in your dust, you'll find NC 28 south a quaint but very straight road. Don't be fooled; just over the first rise, the road spins into a series of wicked switchbacks and hairpin turns. These are punctuated by the scenery off to the right side of the road. One of those mountains off on your right is Wayah Bald. You'll be tearing your way up that mountain in a while. For now, concentrate on the well-banked curves of NC 28 as they lead you to Franklin.

If one of your riding buddies inexplicably exclaims, "Let's go to Jail!" don't assume that he's a candidate for the loony bin. He just might be talking about the Old Jail Gem & Mineral Museum in Franklin. Having served its time housing prisoners, this old jail now houses, sells, and displays gems and minerals, and tells the history of gem and mineral mining in the region. Open May to October, 10 am to 4 pm, admission is free. Getting there from the ride is easy. Turn right to Main St., then take the first left and go one block. Turn left on Palmer St. and then left on Phillips St. The museum is on the left.

The ride leads you through Franklin by turning right onto Main St., then left at the first traffic light, then right onto Palmer St., which becomes the Old Murphy Highway. Follow the Old Murphy Highway to Wayah Rd., where you'll be turning right at the Phillips 66 gas station.

Wayah Rd. rolls through some pretty farm country before the trees begin to shade the road in a green canopy. It then follows Wayah Creek, climbing toward Wayah Bald. Watch for hairpin turns and sweeping curves.

At mile 35.3 you'll have reached Wayah Crest. Dual-sportbikers can turn right here onto a dirt road and follow it about seven miles to the Wayah Bald fire tower. The 360-degree views are nice, but not worth the trip unless your bike is designed for it.

Just past Wayah Crest is a big surprise. Nantahala Lake, with a shoreline stretching over 29 miles long, seems out of place way up here. But the views of the jagged mountain peaks and flat lake make a remarkably beautiful contrast you're sure to enjoy. Nantahala Lake spills down the west side of Wayah Bald and flows into the Nantahala Gorge.

You'll probably spot people fly-fishing on the Upper Nantahala before Wayah Rd. ends at US 74. Once on US 74, rafters and canoeists dominate the river and the road, so use caution. US 74 follows the Nantahala River downstream to the Nantahala Outdoor Center (NOC) at mile 62, offering

---

TOTAL DISTANCE
48.7 miles

TIME FRAME
1½ hours from start to finish. Add time for taking in views of Nantahala Lake and River or stopping in the gorge for food or a great cup of coffee.

---

adventures in rafting, canoeing, and mountain biking. If you've got time and a few bucks, give the Nantahala River a try. It's a fun raft trip on hot summer days.

Perhaps you're simply hungry. Stop at NOC's River's End Restaurant for a table with great views of the river. The tasty burgers and sandwiches will keep you coming back for more. Across the river and up the hill is Relia's Garden Restaurant, offering gourmet cuisine and a cozy, lodge-like atmosphere. If you like wine or beer with dinner, bring it. They will cork it for you, but won't sell you any.

From NOC, begin the climb out of the Nantahala Gorge. On your left at Kim's Espresso, Books & Music, you'll find more than just a cup of coffee—there are smoothies and internet access, too. Get a drink, log on, and brag about this ride you're doing!

Before US 74 turns back into a four-lane divided road, you'll pass the Nantahala Village Resort. This place is an institution in the area.

The Nantahala Village Resort is the last you'll see of the Nantahala Gorge until you return. The next intersection is US 74/NC 28 north. This is not the end of the ride; that comes in just three more miles at the intersection US 74/NC 28 south.

RIDE ALTERNATIVES

Visiting the Franklin Gem & Mineral Museum in the Old Jail requires leaving the planned route for a couple of blocks. To get there, turn right onto Main St., take the first left, another left onto Palmer St. then another left onto Phillips St. The Museum will be on the left. Later on, ride up the dirt road to the Wayah Bald fire tower at mile 35.3, but don't ride this dirt road unless you're on a dual-sportbike.

ROAD CONDITIONS

All these roads have clean, well-banked asphalt, and most hazards are well marked. In the town of Franklin, Main St. is one-way, heading west. To go east, take the one-way Palmer St. The ride off Wayah Rd. to the Wayah Bald fire tower is rough dirt. It's worth the ride on a dual-sport, but on any other kind of bike the views aren't worth the beating you'll take.

POINTS OF INTEREST

The curves of NC 28 south, the Gem & Mineral Museum at the Old Jail in Franklin, Wayah Bald (picnic area and fire tower), Nantahala Lake and Gorge.

RESTAURANTS

The best restaurants are near the ride's end in the Nantahala Gorge. NOC's **River's End Restaurant** at mile 62 has river views and burgers that are as good as the scenery. Or cross the bridge over the Nantahala River at mile 62.1 to reach **Relia's Garden**, a gourmet restaurant situated on a hill overlooking a flower garden. Try **Kim's** at mile 64.6, for coffee and fruit smoothies on hot summer days, and internet access as well. **Nantahala Village Resort** at mile 66.1 offers breakfast, lunch, dinner, rooms, and cabins, too. This resort has proven itself to be very motorcycle-friendly.

DETAILED DIRECTIONS

MILE 0—Turn onto NC 28 south. *Watch for the hairpin curves in the first mile!*

MILE 21.1—Turn right on Main St. in downtown Franklin. *Or, take in the Franklin Gem & Mineral Museum in the Old Jail. To get there from this intersection, turn right, then take the first left, turn left onto Palmer St. and then left again onto Phillips St. The museum will be on the left.*

MILE 21.2—Turn left at the first intersection.

MILE 21.3—Turn right onto Palmer St., which becomes the Old Murphy Road.

MILE 26.1—Turn right onto Wayah Rd. (there's a Phillips 66 station there). *The Wayah Crest Picnic Area is on the left at mile 35.5 and the "don't-do-it-without-a-dual-sportbike" dirt road leading to the Wayah Bald fire tower is just across the road. Don't miss the nice view of Nantahala Lake at mile 43.*

MILE 54.6—Turn right onto US 74 when Wayah Rd. ends. *There's a river launch site there and a roadside river overlook just south of this intersection. At mile 62 is River's End Restaurant with tasty burgers and sandwiches with good views of the Nantahala. Across the river and up the hill is Relia's Garden Restaurant. Kim's Espresso, Books & Music is at mile 64.6, offering coffee, smoothies, and internet access. Nantahala Village Resort offers nice rooms, cabins, and a fantastic restaurant at mile 66.1.*

MILE 70—The ride ends where it began. *Stay on US 74 north to reach I-40, or go south to head toward Murphy.*

Franklin Loop

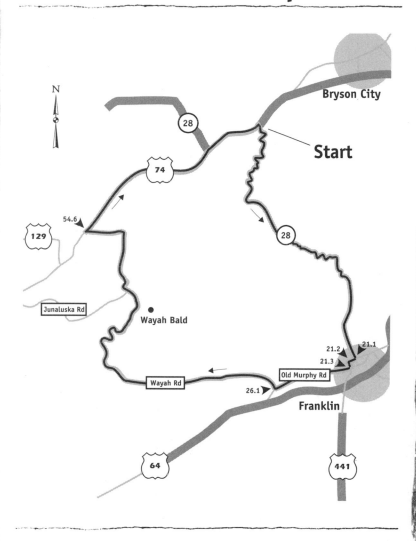

N

Bryson City

28

74

Start

54.6

129

28

Junaluska Rd

Wayah Bald

21.1
21.2
21.3

Old Murphy Rd

Wayah Rd

26.1

Franklin

64

441

75 Interstate Highway	**28** NC State Highway	▬▬ Route
27 US Highway	**91** TN, VA, SC State Highway	▬▬ Other Road
	5 ▶ Milepost	▬▬ Blue Ridge Parkway

The High Country

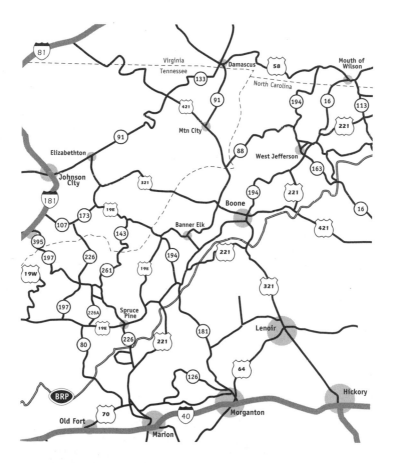

From the mile-high spectacle of Grandfather Mountain to the murder mystery of the tiny town of Kona, the North Carolina High Country holds many natural, historic, and recreational attractions. It's all just off the Blue Ridge Parkway, with its sweeping curves and astounding views. Enjoy!

Area Covered

Little Switzerland Loop

I t's time for the secret of NC 80 to come out. Not many bikers have known about this hidden treasure, but its curves and scenery are too nice to be kept under wraps any longer. Here it leads to the Blue Ridge Parkway in a series of hairpin turns. The scenery and excellent road conditions of the Blue Ridge Parkway are no secret to anyone, but yet another road on this route, NC 226A, is still unknown to many. Since NC 226 was built, old NC 226A is rarely used. Deemed "too twisty" by many drivers, it has been all but abandoned. This short ride offers everything to the biker on the go—good scenery, fun roads and plenty of food.

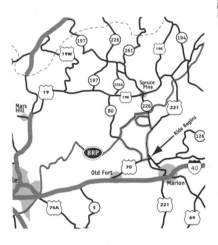

GAS

Gas is available at the start and at miles 1.8 and 35.3, and is abundant on US 221.

GETTING TO THE START

The ride begins just a few minutes off I-40 in Marion, at the intersection of US 70 and US 221. From points west of Marion, take I-40 east to exit 72 in Old Fort, NC and follow US 70 to the ride's start. From points east of Marion, take I-40 west to exit 86 (NC 226) and go north. It will lead you to US 221 north and onto the start of the ride.

RIDE OVERVIEW

This ride begins on a relatively boring stretch of US 70, but as soon as you turn onto NC 80, the road flows next to Buck Creek, twisting its way toward the Blue Ridge Parkway. After passing the very pretty Lake Tahoma, your bike will be thrown into a series of heinous hairpin turns so tight they make the local hairdressers green with envy. Upon reaching Buck Creek Gap and the Blue Ridge Parkway, you'll begin a short but scenic sample of the Parkway.

On the Parkway, watch your speed; the rangers will. Besides, if you go really fast, won't you miss the scenery? Heading north on the Parkway, you'll pass the Black Mountain Overlook, the Three Knob Overlook, and the Crabtree Meadows Store. This store is seasonal and offers some snacks, but don't expect any warm entrees. Save your appetite for Little Switzerland.

For being such a "little" place, Little Switzerland offers grand accommodations, superb dining, and a quaint atmosphere. The Switzerland

Inn sits at the intersection of the Blue Ridge Parkway and NC 226A and has a restaurant, lounge, and rooms with great views. It's a seasonal inn, so if you're interested in staying there, call ahead for information at 800-654-4026, or find it on the web at switzerlandinn.com. Around the corner is the Little Switzerland Cafe. This café offers burgers and sandwiches with a hearty mountain atmosphere. There is a bookstore and general store right next door.

If you take the ride alternative and go north on NC 226A, you'll find the Big Lynn Lodge on the right in just a mile or so. This lodge is open year-round and describes itself as motorcycle-friendly. Its restaurant makes a good breakfast, and dinner is a homestyle, single-entree menu. Reservations for lodging are recommended, and calling ahead to see what's for dinner is a smart idea (828-765-4257 or on the web at biglynnlodge.com). Will you get to meet "Big Lynn"? Sorry, Big Lynn is dead—and it was old age, not obesity, that got her. Contrary to what the name implies, she wasn't a large woman, she was a tree which, until 1965, had stood next to the road we now call NC 226A since before the Revolutionary War. Two of Big Lynn's saplings continue her fine tradition of providing shade for motorcyclists.

From Little Switzerland NC 226A follows Three Mile Creek down the mountain. This road is used much less than NC 226 because NC 226A is just too curvy and steep for commercial traffic. So, that makes NC 226A a great road for bikers, right? Almost, but not quite. Because it's so old, the pavement needs attention, but that is a small price to pay to avoid the 15 mph speed limit imposed on the commercial trucks descending on NC 226 (with no passing lanes to boot!).

TOTAL DISTANCE
42.2 miles

TIME FRAME
1½ hours from start to finish. Add time for chowing down in Little Switzerland.

As NC 226A meets up with NC 226, you'll continue straight onto NC 226 headed toward US 221. Once you reach US 221, turn right to head to the ride's end in Marion. This section is four-lane, straight, and a little dull. What you will see here is stack-stone quarries, and lots of stack stone.

When the ride ends in Marion, you might decide to take in some more riding. The Lake Lure Loop is another short loop ride that starts just a half-hour away in Asheville. Whatever you decide to do, make taking this book with you part of your decision, in case you get a hankering for more motorcycle adventures.

Big Lynn Lodge in Little Switzerland.

RIDE ALTERNATIVES

To avoid the tight twists and ancient pavement of NC 226A, turn north on NC 226A in Little Switzerland. This will take you past the Big Lynn Lodge and then to NC 226 south.

ROAD CONDITIONS

The US routes in this ride are in excellent shape, but lack any curves or views to make them notable. NC 80, the Blue Ridge Parkway, and NC 226A are extremely twisty and have an occasional piece of loose gravel for you to contend with. NC 80 also has a few spots of exposed tar, making it a slick ride during fog, rain, or snow (if you're so inclined). A note about the alternate route: NC 226 is a freshly paved road in excellent condition, but it is used by commercial traffic with a speed limit of 15 mph. With no passing lanes and lots of well-banked curves, this section of NC 226 can be a real challenge to your nerves.

POINTS OF INTEREST

The views of Lake Tahoma; the curves of NC 80; views from Black Mountain Overlook, Three Knob Overlook, and Deer Lick Gap; the town of Little Switzerland (food, lodging, general store, and even a bookstore).

RESTAURANTS

In Marion, **fast food** shops are abundant. If you can last about 45 minutes, try the fare at the **Switzerland Inn**, the **Little Switzerland Cafe** or the **Big Lynn Lodge**. The **Switzerland Inn** (www.switzerlandinn.com or 800-654-4026) has a lounge for informal dining, but the restaurant beckons you to enjoy its food and spectacular views. This inn offers lodging with a European flare. If a quick sandwich is what you want and you can dispense

with scenery for a little while, the **Little Switzerland Café** is your place. For mountainside dining and/or lodging, try the **Big Lynn Lodge** (828-765-4257, or www.biglynnlodge.com). This lodge is not named for a fat lady, but rather for a large tree that provided shelter to soldiers during the Revolution. The tree died in 1965, but her two "kids" are growing where she fell.

DETAILED DIRECTIONS

MILE 0—Head west on US 70 from its intersection with US 221 in Marion. *You'll see a Wal-Mart at this intersection.*

MILE 1.8—Turn Right onto NC 80. *Lake Tahoma will greet you at mile 4.3.*

MILE 14—Go north on the Blue Ridge Parkway. *This is the eastern Continental Divide at 3,350 ft. Take advantage of the three scenic overlooks on the Parkway or stop in at the Crabtree Meadows Store.*

MILE 24.4—Exit the Blue Ridge Parkway in Little Switzerland. Head south on NC 226A. *Enjoy the General Store, cafe, and bookstore in Little Switzerland. There's also nice lodging, food, and drinks at the Switzerland Inn on NC 226A at the Blue Ridge Parkway. The ride alternative starts here; take 226A north to NC 226 south. This route will take you past the Big Lynn Lodge.*

MILE 34.1—Continue straight when NC 226A meets NC 226.

MILE 35.3—Turn right onto US 221 south.

MILE 42.2—The ride ends where it began at the intersection of US 221 and US 70. *Take US 70 west to hit I-40 west and on to Asheville, or follow US 221 south through Marion to I-40 east toward Hickory.*

Little Switzerland Loop

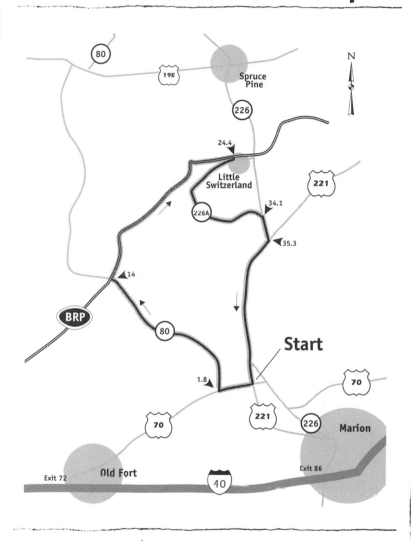

Start

Burnsville Loop

With very little traffic on little-known roads, this ride flows alongside several rivers and streams as it twists and turns through part of the Pisgah National Forest. Because traffic is so sparse, these narrow winding roads have not been abused, leaving them in worry-free condition. Burnsville Loop is an excellent introduction to several secluded mountain towns.

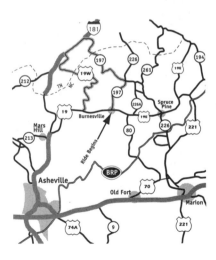

GETTING TO THE START

This ride starts on NC 197 north off US 19W in Burnsville. To get there from Asheville, take US 19/23 north from Asheville and follow US 19 after it splits with US 23. The left turn onto NC 197 north is just 17.7 miles beyond the split. Reset your trip meter as you turn north onto NC 197.

RIDE OVERVIEW

As soon as you turn north onto NC 197 from US 19, you'll notice a lack of commercial structures. Gone are the gas stations and barbershops. In their places are small rustic homes next to a wild ribbon of roadway. NC 197 runs through the Green Mountains and then to the Toe River. You'll cross the Toe River on an old dilapidated bridge that was built in the 1950s. During that era of road-building, the motto for the North Carolina DOT was "Get the farmer out of the mud." True to its mission, it got the farmer out of the mud, but onto a bridge that is failing the test of time. NC 197 continues north, following the banks of the river. NC 197 "T"s into NC 226 in the town of Red Hill.

In Red Hill, you'll find a gas station and little else. After joining with NC 226 for just a tenth of a mile or so, NC 197 forks off to the left and follows the Nolichucky River on its way to the Tennessee State Line. The road then pierces the barrier of the Unaka Mountains through one of the gaps in this small range. Once in Tennessee, NC 197 becomes TN 395. Over the state line, the road surface shows a little less age as you make

GAS
Gas is available at the start in Burnsville and at miles 14.7, 32.5, 32.7, and 33.5.

your way to Rock Creek and Erwin. The towns of Rock Creek and Erwin are very close neighbors. In fact, the town boundary line is indiscernible to a passing biker. One line that's easy to see is between the country restaurants in Rock Creek and the popular fast food joints of Erwin. For a taste of local dining, try the Park Place Restaurant, offering friendly, country-style service. Open for breakfast, lunch, and dinner most days, this little-known gem is a real treat to visit.

Once TN 395 ends at TN 107, this ride makes a left turn toward Erwin, where there's plenty of fuel and fast food. The route makes a right at the Erwin City Hall to remain on TN 107.

You'll cross the railroad tracks, and then you're just a curve or two from the interstate-like US 19W/23. Follow this interstate section, southbound, only to the next exit. At the next exit, follow the signs for US 19W south. Just before entering the thick woods, notice the sign warning truckers of the tight twist and turns. Signs like that read like an invitation to motorcyclists!

Don't assume that because US 19W is a US route, it has fewer curves than its state and county road counterparts. US 19W has its own share of twisties and sweeping curves. This part of the ride will take you alongside the banks of Spivey Creek through the Pisgah National Forest. There's a gravel pullout (just big enough for a bike or two, thanks) next to Spivey Falls, a small waterfall with a huge cooling effect, even on the hottest summer days.

TOTAL DISTANCE
70 miles

TIME FRAME
2 ½ hours from start to finish. Add time to eat in Erwin or to picnic along Spivey Creek or in Pisgah National Forest.

You'll spin through a few more twists and turns as you meander your way back into North Carolina. Once in North Carolina, US 19W follows the Cane River toward Burnsville. Along the way, you're sure to notice the pedestrian bridges that stretch from each home across the Cane to US 19W. Many of these homes have driveways that ford the river. During times of heavy rain, the fords become too deep to drive across, so they had to have an alternate way across the river. Swinging pedestrian bridges provide a necessary alternative as well as adding a unique flavor to the local landscape.

All too soon, US 19W meets US 19, and the ride ends. Turn right to head south on US 19 and back toward Asheville, or turn left to head through Burnsville to Spruce Pine, Banner Elk, and Boone.

RIDE ALTERNATIVES

If you find yourself in Erwin, TN and your time is running low, or you've grown tired of negotiating twists and turns, you can stay on US 23 and follow it all the way back into North Carolina and to points farther south (like Asheville). This will cut an hour off the trip time. US 23 is a divided four-lane most of the way. In North Carolina, there is a section that is not yet four-lane, but they're working to change that.

ROAD CONDITIONS

Tight twists and turns and a few sweeping curves dominate this ride. You'll find little in the way of signage to warn you about approaching hazards, so expect the road ahead to bend sharply. Mostly fresh, clean asphalt, this route has very few places to worry about, but watch for the occasional piece of gravel. During most of the year, traffic is light and is made up only of the local residents going to and returning from civilization. In early November, the roads get busy with commercial trucks transporting Christmas trees, the local commodity, to market.

POINTS OF INTEREST

The Toe, Nolichucky, and Cane Rivers; Spivey Creek (with Spivey Falls); and many fun twists and turns along the way.

RESTAURANTS

The **Park Place Restaurant** in Rock Creek, TN, at mile 30.8 is open from 7 am to 9 pm, seven days a week. The breakfast menu's most popular item is the homemade biscuits and gravy. For lunch, try a cheeseburger with fries for about $5. The dinner menu is similar to the lunch menu, but on Friday and Saturday nights you can order the chef's special of the night, typically something like a T-bone steak ($12) or fried catfish ($9).

There's plenty of **fast food** in Erwin, TN. Get your burger to go and dine next to Spivey Falls.

DETAILED DIRECTIONS

MILE 0—Turn north onto NC 197 from US 19E. *(You might see NC 197 north directly off US 19/23 on a map about 40 miles to the south. DON'T GO THAT WAY! It will take you to Burnsville, but only by way of a long gravel road.)* At

mile 10.5, you'll cross the Toe River on a dilapidated 1950s vintage bridge.

MILE 11.2—NC 197 "T"s into NC 226. Turn left.

MILE 11.3—Make an immediate left onto NC 197. *At mile 17.3, there is a well-marked fork in the road; bear left. Cross the railroad tracks at mile 18.2. After crossing the Nolichucky River at mile 20.7, turn left to remain on NC 197. Hit Tennessee at mile 26.3, where NC 197 becomes TN 395. The views through the Unaka Mountains are spectacular. You'll enter the area of Rock Creek and Erwin, TN. The Park Place Restaurant is at mile 30.8.*

MILE 32.5—TN 395 ends into TN 107. Turn left. *There's fast food just a block or two to the right.*

MILE 33.5—Turn right to remain on TN 107.

MILE 34—Take the entrance ramp onto US 19W/23. *This section is a four-lane divided highway.*

MILE 40—Take exit #12 to US 19W south. *Turn left off the exit ramp.*

MILE 40.3—Following the signs for US 19W, turn right.

MILE 41.5—Turn left to remain on US 19W. *Enjoy the warning sign to truckers about switchbacks on US 19W. See Spivey Falls from a small gravel pullout on the right side of the road at mile 45.8. You'll reenter North Carolina at mile 48.*

MILE 69.6—Follow the signs and turn right to remain on US 19W.

MILE 70—This ride ends at the intersection of US 19W and US 19. *Turn left to return to Burnsville, or right to follow US 19 back south toward Asheville.*

Burnsville Loop

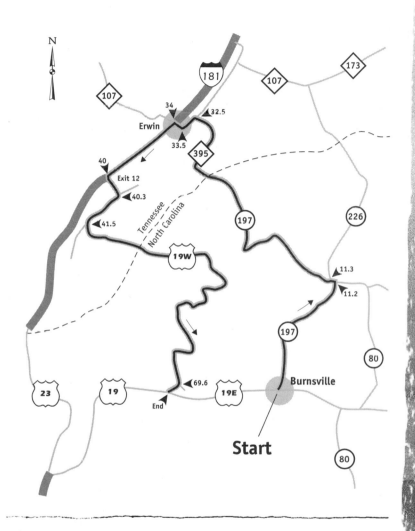

The map includes the following labels and markers:

- N (compass)
- 107 (TN, VA, SC State Highway)
- 181 (Interstate Highway)
- 107
- 173
- 34
- 32.5
- Erwin
- 33.5
- 395
- 40
- Exit 12
- 40.3
- 197
- 226
- 41.5
- Tennessee / North Carolina
- 19W
- 11.3
- 11.2
- 197
- 80
- 69.6
- 23
- 19
- End
- 19E
- Burnsville
- 80

Start

Legend

75 Interstate Highway	28 NC State Highway	▬▬ Route
27 US Highway	91 TN, VA, SC State Highway	— Other Road
	5 ▶ Milepost	═══ Blue Ridge Parkway

Murder Mountain

No, there's no "Murder Mountain" in western North Carolina. This ride derives its name from two interesting sites you'll pass along the route. The "Murder" half of the name comes from the macabre story you'll learn about as you twist your way north on NC 80 through the town of Kona. The "Mountain" along this route is Roan Mountain. Roan Mountain climbs to the staggering elevation of 6,267 ft. above sea level.

As if the mountain scenery and a little murder mystery weren't enough, the roads and the superb views are the real stars of this ride. Seldom used by commercial traffic, the routes chosen for this ride are twisty, clean, and fun to ride on any kind of motorcycle!

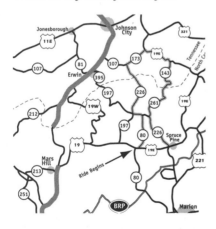

GAS
Gas is available at miles 16.1, 20.2, 24, 31.6, 46.1, 51.6, 65.8, 72, and 72.6.

GETTING TO THE START

This ride starts on NC 80 off US 19E between Spruce Pine and Burnsville, NC. From Asheville, you'll go north on US 19 out of town and follow the signs onto 19E. From elsewhere use I-40, take exit 85 (US 221, town of Marion), head north on US 221 into Spruce Pine, then turn west onto US19E. Reset your trip meter as you turn onto NC 80 north from US 19E.

RIDE OVERVIEW

Turning north onto NC 80 from US 19E, you'll first notice the sound of silence. Gone is the heavy commercial traffic that littered US 19E. NC 80 will twist you through several small towns as you drive its 13-mile length. If you ride this route soon enough, you might drive across a rickety old bridge built in 1922, condemned in 1952, but still in use because, as one local said, "What choice do we have?" To answer the public's demand for a new bridge, the NC DOT is constructing a new $51,000,000 bridge that will replace both the vehicle bridge and the rail bridge. Look for the new bridge to be completed by 2003.

Just past the bridge is the quaint town of Kona. Kona was a feldspar mining town until the EPA shut the mine down in 1958 because the townspeople were suffering from "white lung." As you ride through Kona, you'll see a cemetery and small church on the right side of the road. That small church has no door locks and the respectful public is always welcome. Kona isn't famous for its many years of mining. Kona gained its notoriety for being the hometown of the first woman ever to be hanged in North Carolina. So, what evil did she commit?

Charlie Silver was the son of a revolutionary war hero. The family's cabin still sits in the valley in the town of Kona. It was built in 1794 and still stands as one of the largest homes in Kona with the two stories and two chimneys. Charlie was a young man when he met Frankie. She was a slight girl, just barely five feet tall and not weighing more than 90 lbs. Cupid's arrow struck the teenage couple and soon they were married. What happened one cold winter just three days before Christmas in 1831 is not entirely known, but what is known is that Frankie killed Charlie with an ax. She was so enraged that she cut him into little bits and scattered him around the town and local hills. Frankie was arrested and put on trial. While awaiting trial, the townspeople found what they thought was all of Charlie and buried him in the church yard. Well, after the funeral, a few more parts of Charlie were found. In

TOTAL DISTANCE
81.5 miles

TIME FRAME
3 hours from start to finish. Add time for stops, and add a half hour if you plan to visit the town of Kona or any of the attractions on Roan Mountain.

an effort to preserve the dignity of Charlie's grave site, they dug a new grave and buried Charlie's newfound parts next to the others. A few days later, they found still more of Charlie and did the same thing. Poor Charlie is buried in three separate grave sites! What price did his young bride pay for her crime? She received the dubious distinction of being the first woman hanged in North Carolina. The folks of Kona still say that after she was hanged, the State of North Carolina made eight burial sites for Frankie, in an effort to prevent the Silver family from mutilating her body and scattering it. Bottom line for this macabre story? One couple with eleven burial sites.

You'll find Charlie Silver's graves in the cemetery behind the Kona Church.

There's not much left of Bandana save the sign.

Today, Kona is home to the Mountain Hill Country Gallery. If you appreciate art, stop in and check out some of the local talent. Kona is so small, you won't need directions to the gallery. You'll see it from anywhere in Kona.

Twisting past Kona, NC 80 takes you through the town of Bandana. Bandana's name is derived from the method people used there for flagging down the train. Because the town wasn't a regular stop, the train's conductor would only stop if he saw someone waving a red bandana. Now you know!

NC 80 ends at its intersection with NC 226. Turn left there. Just around the corner from this turn you'll enter the town of Loafer's Glory and see the Bonnie and Clyde Drive Inn. At Bonnie and Clyde's you can have a burger and fries or you might elect to have a simple cup of coffee. No, Bonnie and

Clyde's Drive Inn was not named after the gangsters, but rather the original owners, who by all accounts weren't gangsters at all. The reasonable prices prove there's no highway robbery in Loafer's Glory.

After leaving Loafer's Glory, NC 226 turns into a roller-coaster of a highway. With dips and twists leading you through this tree-canopied highway, you'll be taking in some of the best scenery in the Pisgah National Forest. There's no fanfare at the state line; only two simple signs followed by the dreaded state highway renumbering game. NC 226 becomes TN 107.

Shortly after entering Tennessee, you emerge from the heavy woods into pastureland. TN 107 offers a few straightaways as you reach the next turn onto TN 173. At this juncture in the ride you'll find the Creekside Restaurant, offering breakfast, lunch, and dinner. It ain't fancy, but it sho' is good!

After leaving the restaurant, you'll discover that TN 173 gives you several sweeping turns to ease the digestion process. Nearly flat, TN 173 leads you to US 19E alongside a creek bed.

Turning on US 19E, you may assume that this ride is nearly over because US 19E looks like a giant slab of asphalt and offers nothing for the motorcyclist. Look again as you climb toward Roan Mountain. Upon closer inspection, you'll see this section of US 19E is very motorcycle-friendly. With ample truck lanes and passing lanes, it's a real ride-saver.

In the town of Roan Mountain, TN, you're going to be turning right onto TN 143. This road will lead you on a twisty and scenic climb up Roan

Mountain. If you have a minute or you have a week, stop in at the Roan Mountain State Park Visitor Center. There you'll find a gift shop, a few vending machines, and information about camping, hiking, renting cabins. Last but certainly not least, the "Peg Leg Iron Ore Mine" is complete with its own sluice and water wheel.

Leaving the iron ore where you left it and proceeding up NC 143, you and your bike will be tossed through a set of twists and turns that will make even the toughest biker crack a joyful smile. At the top of Roan Mountain you'll discover the Roan Mountain Information Center, the Rhododendron Garden, the Appalachian Trail, and the entire state of North Carolina hiding just around the next curve. Again the road gets renumbered to NC 261.

What comes up must come down, and that's exactly what you'll do for the next half hour as you ride down the North Carolina side of Roan Mountain. On this side of the mountain, the road cuts between Pumpkin Patch Mountain and Fork Mountain. Because of this there are few distant vistas, but the beauty of this little road is all in its design. Offering plenty of well-banked curves and clean asphalt, it's a pleasure to ride as you cruise into the town of Bakersville.

In Bakersville, you'll continue straight onto NC 226 which will descend all the way back toward Spruce Pine where the ride ends at US 19E. If you're not ready to quit, don't despair; your adventures can continue from here. You can join in on the Little Switzerland Loop just a few miles south of Spruce Pine off NC 226. Or, you might decide to head to ski country and take in the Banner Elk ride. Either way, there's still plenty of road left to ride.

The approach road to Roan Mountain begins at Carvers Gap on the Tennessee/North Carolina border.

RIDE ALTERNATIVES

You can shave about half an hour off this ride by avoiding NC 80. Do this by starting the ride on NC 226 north from US 19E, just west of Spruce Pine. In doing so, you'll rejoin the ride at mile 13 of the route at the intersection of NC 80 and NC 226.

ROAD CONDITIONS

Except for a short stretch of US 19E, all the roads used for this route are seldom used by commercial traffic. While the hazards are well marked on TN 143 and NC 261 over Roan Mountain, the same cannot be said of NC 80 and the northern stretch of NC 226. Watch for tight, unmarked twists on NC 80 and NC 226. The asphalt is in excellent condition with the occasional piece of gravel to keep your attention.

POINTS OF INTEREST

The town of Kona, with its cemetery, small church, and the artist's gallery. Roan Mountain State Park (TN) and the Roan Mountain Rhododendron Gardens and Information Center atop Roan Mountain.

RESTAURANTS

In Loafer's Glory, you'll find **Bonnie and Clyde's Drive Inn** offering great eats at low prices. If you make it into Tennessee before your stomach begins to make demands, try stopping at the **Creekside Restaurant** at the intersection of TN 107 and TN 173. They are open for breakfast, lunch, and dinner and even offer milkshakes!

DETAILED DIRECTIONS

MILE 0—Turn onto NC 80 north from US 19E. *At mile 2.5 is the circa 1922 bridge, but better get there fast; the new bridge will be finished soon! The macabre story of the town of Kona unfolds before your eyes at mile 5.8.*

MILE 10.8—Make a left to stay on NC 80 (it's well marked).

MILE 13—NC 80 ends at NC 226; make a left. *In Loafer's Glory you'll find Bonnie and Clyde's Drive Inn. Good food and the prices aren't highway robbery! At mile 17.9 a footbridge crosses Rock Creek. You'll enter Tennessee at mile 27 where the road becomes TN 107.*

MILE 31.6—Turn right onto TN 173. *If you have a minute and you're hungry, try the Creekside Restaurant.*

MILE 38.3—Turn right onto US 19E. *Enjoy these passing lanes.*

MILE 46.1—Turn right onto TN 143 and begin your ascent up Roan Mountain. *Stop in at the Roan Mountain State Park Visitor Center at mile 48.1. There's an iron ore mine, vending machines, restrooms, and a gift shop. You can check in here for camping and cabins (better call ahead for the cabin reservations at 800-250-8620). Nice roadside toilet at mile 55. At mile 59.1, you will have reached Carvers Gap elevation 5,512 ft. and the North Carolina State Line. Turn right here to get to the Rhododendron Gardens and the Roan Mountain Information Center. TN 143 becomes NC 261.*

MILE 72—NC 261 meets NC 226 in the town of Bakersville; go straight onto NC 226 south.

MILE 81.5—The ride ends where NC 226 meets US 19E just west of Spruce Pine.

Murder Mountain

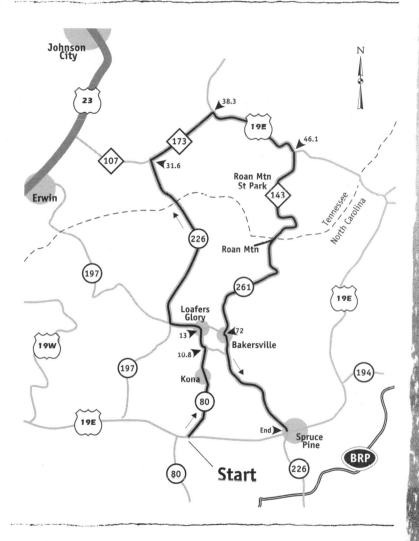

Boone & Banner Elk

Starting in Boone and passing through the small burgs of Valle Crucis, Banner Elk, Cranberry, Minneapolis, Plumtree, and others, this route passes many historic and scenic areas in North Carolina. Along the way, the road twists wildly, and you'll be along for the ride! Be sure to visit the original Mast General Store, the ski slopes of Beech Mountain, several good restaurants, and even an abandoned Hollywood movie set.

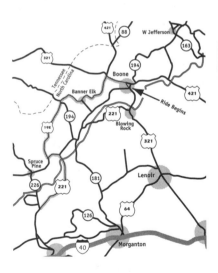

GAS

Gas is plentiful at the start of the ride in Boone and is also available at miles 5.6, 18.2, 23, 25.3, 38.1, 38.3, 46, 47.9, 56.3, and 62.

GETTING TO THE START

This ride starts in the heart of Boone at the intersection of US 321/221 and NC 105 (that's the intersection with the two-story Wendy's). Many roads lead to Boone. From the south you can take US 321 north from I-40 in Hickory, or US 221 north from Marion. If you're headed to Boone from Tennessee, take US 421 south from I-40, near Bristol. Either way, zero your trip meter as you turn north on US 221 from the intersection of US 321/221 and NC 105.

RIDE OVERVIEW

Begin in the heart of Boone. Named for the legendary mountain man Daniel Boone, the town is a popular tourist destination year-round. In the summer, it is occupied by motorcyclists and outdoor adventurers. In the winter, skiers take advantage of Boone's proximity to several ski slopes. You'll ride north on US 221 from the intersection of US 221, US 321, and NC 105. In just under a mile, you'll reach a "T" intersection, where you'll make a left onto US 421 north. This stretch of road will lead you through the old business district of Boone, where you'll find some cool places to eat—like a bagel shop and a soda fountain in the drugstore. The Boone Mast General Store is on the right side of the road. Peek through the window as you pass it; you're going to visit the original Mast store later. A couple of blocks off to the left is Appalachian State University.

After leaving Boone, you'll be making a left onto NC 194 south.

Beyond the turn, a sign warns drivers that the road ahead is so twisty that vehicles over 35 ft. are not recommended. It fails to mention that motorcyclists will greatly enjoy the road. You'll immediately be flung through several tight and narrow turns. The road surface is a little rough, but the turns are so tight, you won't need a lot of throttle anyway.

About four miles into your journey down NC 194, you'll enter the town of Valle Crucis. It gets its name from the Latin words meaning "Vale of the Cross." The town was created as a religious retreat, and flourished. Then it really got a boost when Mr. W.W. Mast built a general store.

On the left side of the road is where you'll find Mast General Store. Opened in 1883, they offer everything from "cradles to caskets." The general store has been kept in nearly its original condition. As you walk across the wooden floor, it's easy to imagine the bartering that took place not so long ago. Today, the staff of Mast General Store barter very little—cash and credit cards are accepted over

livestock and labor. But even if you don't plan to buy anything, stop in the Mast General Store to enjoy this landmark while we still have it. Classic general stores in this region are becoming more rare each day. You'll find an example of this later as you ride past the remains of the C.W. Wilson General Store in Plumtree, NC.

A scant block past Mast General Store, the ride makes a right to remain on NC 194. If you miss the right turn, the road changes into Broadstone Rd. and will lead you to NC 105. But you'll want to stay on NC 194 to continue this adventure.

After making the right turn to remain on NC 194, the road becomes

Jars of honey and sacks of seed line the shelves inside Mast General Store.

The sign says it all. Have a good time.

unbelievably narrow and twisty. The locals claim that NC 194 is so twisty that you'll pass the same house three times. While you might not *actually* pass the same house three times, you will negotiate hairpin turn after hairpin turn. Like the earlier portion of NC 194, this section is a little rough and you might find a chunk of gravel in the corners, so watch your speed.

NC 194 will begin to straighten out a little as you near Banner Elk. You won't find any elk in Banner Elk. The town was once known as *Shawneehaw*. The name was changed when the Banner family settled on the banks of the Elk River nearby. The marriage of Banner and Elk has been a good one. For such a microscopic-sized town, it's a big magnet for outdoor adventure types.

In Banner Elk, you'll find a traffic light at the intersection of NC 194 and NC 184 south. At this corner is the aptly named Corner Bar, Corner Palate,

and Corner Grill. Three unique restaurants under one roof! The prices are a bit high, but hey, you're on vacation. About a hundred yards down NC 184 south is the Banner Elk Cafe. You'll enjoy the food and prices at this comparatively inexpensive restaurant and ice cream shop. Just past the Banner Elk Cafe is Racing Station. Racing Station is the local Harley-Davidson accessory distributor. Inside, you'll discover how they came to be known as the Racing Station. Not only is it a Harley accessory store, they also do quite a bit of business selling NASCAR collectibles. If you were to continue down NC 184 south, you'd ride back to NC 105 and the town of Tynecastle, NC.

The route continues on NC 194. As you near the western city limit of Banner Elk, you'll see the Lees McRae College campus on the left side of the road. It's hard to imagine having to concentrate on college courses with so much beauty just outside the classroom. After passing the college, watch for signs for NC 184 north and Beech Mountain. This mountain is home to Ski Beech, a popular ski slope. There's quite a celebration in October when the locals host an Octoberfest, complete with polka bands.

Continuing on NC 194, you'll pass the Elk River airstrip. Not a huge airport, but it's big enough to land the private jets of the rich and famous who come to relax in the arms of North Carolina's High Country.

You'll turn left when NC 194 "T's" into US 19E. You'll follow US 19E a couple of miles and then turn right to remain on US 19E. The road follows the banks of the Toe River through Minneapolis (not Minnesota, but what a great shortcut that would be) and into Plumtree. In Plumtree, you'll see the Plumtree Presbyterian Church on the left and the remains of the C.W. Wilson General Store on the right.

This tiny town enjoyed a brief taste of fame in 1990 when the movie *Winter People* was filmed here. The movie brought Kurt Russell, Kelly McGillis, and other Hollywood stars to Plumtree. The story line followed Russell's character to a small North Carolina town where he falls in love with McGillis's character, who was in the center of a family feud involving her illegitimate child. Russell's character, a clockmaker, creates a clocktower for the town and wins the affection of the town and the girl of his dreams. Today, the stone clocktower stands in the middle of a grassy field near the Toe River. Actually, it's made of fiberglass or some other kind of Hollywood

The "Leaning Tower of Plumtree" sits in a pretty field beside the Toe River.

production goo. Nearby is the ruin of the C.W. Wilson General Store that also starred in the movie.

Built in 1886, the C. W. Wilson General Store provided everything the community needed, including dry goods, a post office, candy, and even a dentist's office (in case you forgot to brush after all that candy). The movie depicted the store as it was in its heyday, with people gathering on the front steps to gossip, shoppers bartering inside, and a friendly staff who knew every customer by name. When the filming ended, the glitz and glamour of Hollywood quickly faded, and the store fell into disrepair. The roof gave way in the mid-1990s. Not wanting to let anything go to waste, enterprising locals scavenged the rare wormy chestnut wood from the dilapidated structure for use as architectural accents in new homes.

Following US 19E across the Toe River, you'll see the Toe River Lodge. This lodge caters to the fly-fishers who take advantage of the Toe's abundant trout population. Most any day, you can spot people standing in the river, whipping their rods to make the flies at the end of their fishing lines dance for the hungry trout in the water below. It's an artful sport.

You'll follow the Toe for a couple more miles as the road begins to settle into a rhythm of sweeping turns. The ride makes a left turn onto Three Mile Highway, sometimes marked as NC 194 north. In a little over four miles ("But I thought this was *Three* Mile Highway," you say), the road "T"s into US 221, where this route turns right. You can make this ride a loop by turning left here and returning to Boone. In doing so, you'll cross over scenic Grandfather Mountain and cut through the quaint vacation town of Blowing Rock. Following this route, make the right turn and head under the Blue Ridge Parkway and into the town of Linville Falls.

The town of Linville Falls derives its name from the waterfall of the same name a couple miles away, where the Linville River cascades 90 ft. through the Linville Gorge. In the town of Linville Falls, the only things cascading are the gasoline as it trickles into your gas tank and the iced tea from the pitchers in two great restaurants.

The restaurants of Linville Falls are Spear's Barbecue and Famous Louise's Rock House Restaurant. Spear's Barbecue is famous for baby back ribs and a long wine and beer list. The menu is extensive, but the ribs are the major attraction. Across the street is Famous Louise's Rock House Restaurant. So far, it's Louise that's famous, but if they keep serving up such delicious country cooking, the food will be more famous than she. Famous Louise's sits on the borders of Avery, Burke, and McDowell Counties. Inside the restaurant, signs hanging from the ceiling let you know which county you're sitting in. Tip well here; it's not unusual for a waitress to have to walk across two county lines just to bring you your lunch!

US 221 begins to descend into the Linville Valley in a series of steep, sweeping turns. Near the bottom of the mountain, signs beckon to the Linville Caverns. The cavern tour lasts just a half-hour as it meanders through the 52-degree cave. The cavern is home to trout, bats, stalagmites, stalactites, and a subterranean stream. Admission is $5. It's a neat place to visit and a great break from the heat on a hot summer day.

Just past the Linville Caverns, US 221 begins to straighten out as you near the ride's end. On a clear day, you'll see Linville Mountain to your left and Hunnicutt Mountain to your right as you roll freely through the Linville Valley on your way to the ride's end. You might encounter some construction in the last few miles of the ride; the DOT is widening part of US 221 from two to four lanes.

The ride ends at the intersection of US 221 and NC 226. You'll have many choices at this intersection. You can turn right and follow NC 226 to the Blue Ridge Parkway or the towns of Spruce Pine and Little Switzerland, or you can continue straight on US 221 into the city of Marion where you'll find US 70 and I-40. Several rides cross through this part of US 221, so be sure to have this book with so you can add some more riding to your day.

The still-standing walls of the C.W. Wilson General Store

The menu at Famous Louise's is plain-looking, but extensive.

RIDE ALTERNATIVES

You can make this a loop ride back to Boone by turning left onto US 221 at mile 46 and following it north past Grandfather Mountain, through Blowing Rock and back into Boone.

ROAD CONDITIONS

This ride has many tight twists and turns, and most of them are unmarked. Because NC 194 is so narrow and windy, there are signs on it warning drivers not to operate vehicles over 35 ft. in length. There are few warning signs to let you know what the road is doing ahead, so plan for a wicked decreasing radius turn. The roads chosen on this route have good asphalt surfaces and are well banked, but the errant piece of gravel sometimes finds its way into the travel lanes.

POINTS OF INTEREST

The Mast General Stores (one in Boone and one in Valle Crucis), the turns on the road to Banner Elk, Harley accessory dealership in Banner Elk, Beech Mountain Ski Area, Elk River airstrip, the site of the filming of the movie *Winter People* in Plumtree, and Linville Caverns.

RESTAURANTS

There are many places to choose from. It's all about what food mood you're in.

In Banner Elk, stop in at the **Corner Bar** to dine in three restaurants all at once. The **Corner Bar** sits at the corner of NC 194 and NC 184 in downtown Banner Elk. This unusual establishment is home to the Corner Bar, the **Corner Palate** and the **Corner Grill**. For about $15, the Grill offers burgers, fries, and a beer for lunch. For dinner, feast on California Seafood at the **Corner Palate** for $28. Sure, there are less expensive items on the menu, but do you really want to eat a $16 pot pie? The Corner Bar offers french fries and other between-meals snacks between lunch and dinner.

If your tastes are limited by your budget, try the **Banner Elk Cafe**. The Café is about 100 yards down NC 184 from NC 194, on the right. Open from 7 am to 9 pm, the Café offers breakfast, lunch, and dinner with menu items for every dining taste and dollar amount. For example, you can have an egg and cheese sandwich for breakfast for just $1.50 or go all-out and have the Mountain Man Special, which is anything and everything you could ever want for breakfast for $7. The lunch menu is just as varied. You can order a small burger for $3.50 or have the 1-lb. burger for $8. Dinner includes Mountain Trout for $12, or a simple veggie plate for $5.

In keeping with the vacation resort theme, there are a couple of coffee shops in Banner Elk. Take a minute or two to explore the downtown on your own. Because Banner Elk is so small, it's mighty easy to explore.

Near the end of the ride in Linville Falls, there's the **Famous Louise's Rock House Restaurant**. For the record, it's Louise who's famous, but her restaurant is quickly catching up.

Famous Louise's sits on the borders of Avery, Burke, and McDowell counties. Inside the restaurant you'll find the county line signs hanging from the ceiling. You'd better tip your waitress well, because she will likely have to walk to Avery County to give the cook your order, pick it up in Burke County, and serve you in McDowell County. What a workout! So what's the food like? Tasty veggies and home-style meals for reasonable prices. Famous Louise's is open for breakfast at 6 am and doesn't close until 8 pm. Across the street from the Rock House is **Spear's Barbecue**, open for lunch and dinner. You'll find burgers and barbecue for lunch; with a beer, plan to drop about $12. For dinner, try the trout for $18. Spear's is sort of like your neighborhood fine dining establishment, but with reasonable prices.

DETAILED DIRECTIONS

MILE 0—Head north on US 221 from the two-story Wendy's.

MILE 0.7—Turn left onto US 421 north (also marked as NC 194 south). *The Boone branch of the Mast General Store is on the right at mile 1.7.*

MILE 6.7—Turn left onto NC 194. *Immediately the road will launch into a steep set of hairpin turns.*

MILE 10.7—Turn right to remain on NC 194 south. *You'll be in Banner Elk around mile 17. At mile 18.2 is the intersection of NC 194 and NC 184. You'll find the Corner Bar at this intersection. Just 100 yards down NC 184 is the Banner Elk Cafe and the Harley accessory dealer. Lees McRae College is on the left as you head out of town on NC 194 south. The road to Beech Mountain is to the right at mile 18.4. What's that piece of asphalt on the left side of the road near mile 18.8? That's the Elk River airstrip.*

MILE 23—NC 194 "Ts" into US 19E. Turn left.

MILE 25.3—Turn right to remain on US 19E. *The chilly town of Minneapolis is at mile 28.5. Find the C.W. Wilson General Store and the movie set/town of Plumtree at mile 36.7. The General Store was torn down in 2001, but pieces of the movie set are still evident (the clocktower is built of fiberglass "stones"). You'll cross the Toe River at mile 36.9, and come to the Toe River Lodge. It's an outdoor store, catering mostly to the fly-fishers that frequent the river.*

MILE 41.8—Turn left onto NC 194 north (also known as Three Mile Highway).

MILE 46—Turn right onto US 221 south. *This is where the ride alternative starts. You can decide to turn left here and head back into Boone via Blowing Rock. You'll cross under the Blue Ridge Parkway at mile 47.1. Spear's Barbecue and Famous Louise's Restaurant are in the town of Linville Falls at mile 47.9. Linville Caverns invites you to tour its deep recesses at mile 51.1.*

MILE 62—The ride ends at the intersection of US 221 and NC 226. *Continue south on US 221 to reach Marion and I-40, or turn right onto NC 226 north to head toward Spruce Pine.*

Boone and Banner Elk

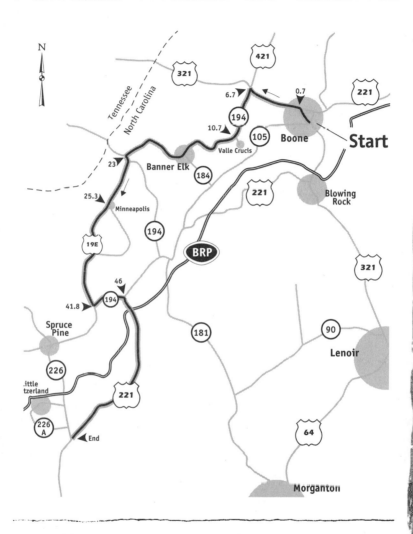

N

Tennessee
North Carolina

321
421
221

6.7
0.7
194
10.7
105
Boone
Start
Valle Crucis
23
Banner Elk
184
25.3
221
Minneapolis
Blowing
Rock
194
BRP
321
19E
46
41.8
194
181
90
Spruce
Pine
Lenoir
226
ittle
tzerland
221
226
A
64
End
Morganton

75 Interstate Highway	28 NC State Highway	▬▬ Route
27 US Highway	91 TN, VA, SC State Highway	— Other Road
	5 ▶ Milepost	═══ Blue Ridge Parkway

Grandfather Loop

Completely circling Grandfather Mountain, this adventure is your introduction to some of the finest roads and attractions in western North Carolina. You can do some caving in the Linville Caverns, dine in three counties all at once, ride a section of the Blue Ridge Parkway over the Lynn Cove Viaduct, visit the Blowing Rock, and investigate a haunted house. With so many things to see and so many towns to visit, plan for a full day of riding.

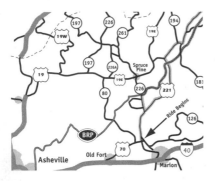

GAS

Gas is as plentiful as the attractions on this ride. You'll find it at the start as well as at miles 1, 2.5, 5.9, 6.7, 12.6, 14.7, and 21; on the side ride to Blowing Rock; at mile 50.1; throughout Boone between miles 51 and 56; at miles 62.2, 63, 65, 67, 74.5, 76.2, 79.7, 81, 82.2, 83.4, 89.7, 91.8, 97.7, 98.5, 101.9, 103.4; and at the ride's end in Marion.

GETTING TO THE START

This ride begins in Marion at the intersection of US 70 and US 221. Marion is just off I-40 (exit 85 is US 221). Take US 221 north from the interstate to the intersection of US 70 and US 221. A more scenic way to get to the start is via US 70 from Old Fort (exit 72 on I-40), going east to Marion. Regardless of how you reach the start, zero your trip meter as you head north on US 221 from US 70.

RIDE OVERVIEW

Starting in Marion, on US 221 north from US 70, the beginning of this adventure offers plenty of fast food, a Wal-Mart, and even a motorcycle dealership. From Mexican fare to baked potatoes, there's fast food for every palate. The Blue Ridge Yamaha dealership is on the right side of US 221 about a half mile north of US 70. Inside, you'll find several bikes, lots of 4x4's, and a few watercraft.

US 221 flows northward as a five-lane road for several miles. Of this ride's 104 miles, this section of US 221 might be the least attractive, but riding still beats working.

Just past the intersection of US 221 and NC 226, the road changes from a large and busy four-lane monstrosity to an invigorating two-lane country road. Until sometime around the summer of 2003, you can expect some construction traffic on the first couple of miles of this two-lane section, because US 221 is getting widened there. Your reward for making it past the construction will be a couple of nice sweeping turns in the shadow of Honeycutt Mountain to your left and Linville Mountain to the right. Next to Honeycutt Mountain is Humpback Mountain. Inside Humpback Mountain is Linville Caverns.

Linville Caverns is a quick and interesting roadside attraction. You'll pay just $5 for a 30-minute tour of the cavern. Inside you'll see stalagmites, stalactites, and fish in a subterranean stream. The temperature in the cavern remains a constant 52 degrees Fahrenheit. During the War between the States, soldiers on both sides deserted the battlefield for the comfort of this cavern.

US 221 becomes decidedly more twisty after passing Linville Caverns, curling your way up to the town of Linville Falls. Linville Falls is so small, you might be inclined to pass it by. Don't. It may be small in size but it's

Linville Falls carves its way through stone at the top of the gorge.

TOTAL DISTANCE
104.4 miles

TIME FRAME
You can finish this ride in 2 hours, or you can plan most of the day to check out the many attractions on the route.

big in hospitality. You'll discover a gas station and two restaurants in town. Spear's Restaurant is popular for its "fall off the bone" baby back ribs and ice cold beer. Famous Louise's Rock House Restaurant is known for tasty home-style meals served in three counties simultaneously. Famous Louise's sits on the borders of Avery, Burke, and McDowell Counties. There are signs hanging from the ceiling indicating in which county you are sitting.

Just through Linville Falls is the entrance to the internationally famous Blue Ridge Parkway. You'll turn off US 221 onto the Blue Ridge Parkway and head north. The Blue Ridge Parkway greets you with several scenic overlooks, attractions, a smooth surface, and sweeping turns. One of the first attractions you'll come to is Linville Falls. No, not the town this time, the actual waterfall. Following the signs from the Parkway onto a side road, you'll ride for a couple of miles to reach an information center and a path to the waterfall. The next attraction is Grandfather Mountain.

The Parkway itself has several overlooks of Grandfather Mountain. Once known to the Cherokee Indians as Tanawha or "Great Hawk" (a name I love), Grandfather Mountain soars to the elevation of 5,964 ft., touted as the highest peak in the Blue Ridge. Sure, there are other mountains in the

Even the stonework along the Parkway is a marvel to look at.

area that are taller. There's Mt. Mitchell at 6,684 ft., tallest east of the Mississippi, but it's in the Black Mountain Range. In the Smoky Mountains, Clingmans Dome is the highest at 6,643 ft. To pay a visit to the top of Grandfather Mountain, you'll need to turn off the Parkway onto US 221 and head up the mountain. It costs $12 to enter this privately owned park, but the views alone are worth the price of admission. After passing through the entrance gate, you'll follow the twisty and steep road past Sphinx and Split Rocks, the Nature Museum and animal habitats (bears, deer, otters, eagles), and end at the Visitor Center and Mile High Swinging Bridge. Take a short walk over the swinging pedestrian bridge onto the craggy precipice overlooking the majesty of the Blue Ridge mountains. The walk back into the Visitor Center from the swinging bridge leads you to the gift shop. There you'll again find the *piece de resistance* of souvenirs everywhere,

the rubber tomahawk. There are also other less cheesy souvenirs to help you recall the fond memories of "Great Hawk" Mountain.

Back on the Parkway, next up is the Lynn Cove Viaduct. If you have time, visit the Lynn Cove Viaduct information center. If you don't have the time, finish reading this paragraph to get the skinny about this quarter mile-long feat of engineering. Completed on September 11, 1987, at a price of $10,000,000, the viaduct was built to minimize the ecological impact to the side of Grandfather Mountain. It is made of 153 concrete segments, only one of which is *not* curved. These segments were manufactured on the side of the mountain. The completion of the Lynn Cove Viaduct also completed the Blue Ridge Parkway. In the 52 years the Parkway had been in existence prior to the construction of the viaduct, riders had to detour from the Parkway onto US 221. Today, the Parkway runs its 469-mile length without interruption.

After crossing the viaduct, you'll be able to catch a few glimpses of it over your shoulder, on your way to Price Lake. Once at Price Lake, you can rent a canoe or rowboat from the Park Service to explore this small lake. Or, simply enjoy the view from the parking/overlook area near the lake's spillway dam.

The Blowing Rock ride starts at mile 45.7 by turning onto US 221 from the Parkway. The town of Blowing Rock offers great restaurants, coffee shops, shopping, and even a true blowing rock. It's said that the snow falls upwards at the Blowing Rock.

On the Parkway, about a half mile from the start of the Blowing Rock ride, is the driveway to the Cone Manor House, also known as Flat Top Manor. Built by textile magnate Moses H. Cone as a retreat from the heat, this estate is open from March 15 to November 30 between the hours of 9 am and 5 pm. This 1900s estate was given to the Park Service by the Cone family after the passing of the elder Cones. Today, the residence is home to a craft and information center. The craft center sells handmade souvenirs and artwork, but no rubber tomahawks. While you're there, keep an eye out for the two ghosts that are believed to haunt the residence. The ghost of Mr. Cone's wife Bertha is thought to wander the estate in protest of the deeding of the estate to the Park Service by the surviving family members. The shade of Bertha's sister, Clementine, is rumored to occupy the house, searching for the out-of-wedlock child she gave up for adoption. Clementine rarely ventures downstairs; she prefers the second story, which is closed to the public.

The ride turns off the Parkway onto the four-lane US 321 north toward Boone. Shortly after turning onto US 321, you'll see the Tweetsie Amusement Park and Railroad. The railroad makes daily trips through the countryside. The amusement park offers several rides and Wild West shows to amuse the visiting crowds.

Named for Daniel Boone, the town of Boone is popular year-round. In the winter, Boone is a destination for skiers and snowboarders. In the summer, people are drawn by the cool temperatures and nearby attractions. You'll find most any kind of food you desire here, but a word to the wise about Boone. Things cost a bit more there, so prepare yourself to pay up to 25% more than you'd expect (the exception is fast food). Hotel rooms

are particularly painful unless you make advance reservations.

The ride makes a left onto NC 105 in the heart of Boone. Many of the other motorcycle adventures start and end at this intersection, so bring this book with you if you think there's a chance you'll want to expand your riding day. NC 105 becomes a two-lane road after passing a couple of miles of Boone businesses. You won't find any tight twists on NC 105, just gentle sweeping curves on the banks of the Watauga River. Along the way, you'll have a great view of grandfather's profile on the top of Grandfather Mountain. It will be on the left side of the road, and takes only a little imagination to see.

Next you'll pass through the town of Tynecastle. Tynecastle is home to several gas stations and businesses, and NC 105 and NC 184 intersect in the center of town. If your plans include a visit to Banner Elk, turn

The footbridge atop Grandfather Mountain is the highest in the East.

The road to the top of Grandfather Mountain is steep and twisty.

right onto NC 184. This is the least curvy way to reach Banner Elk, but it's still a pretty ride.

NC 105 meets US 221 again in Grandfather Village. If you didn't visit Grandfather Mountain earlier in the ride, here's another chance. To get to Grandfather Mountain, turn left from NC 105 onto US 221 and ride the twisty, excellently paved section of US 221 to the Park's entrance about three miles up the mountain. If you've visited Grandfather Mountain and wish to skip it this time, go straight across US 221 from NC 105.

In doing so, you'll be taken from the state road to a quiet county road. You'll pass through a section of beautiful vacation homes, canopied with large trees. All too soon, the county road ends at US 221. The ride makes a left and continues south on US 221.

US 221 leads you back toward the

Blue Ridge Parkway and the town of Linville Falls through some rolling hills and sweeping curves. The last 20 miles of the ride cover the same ground as the first twenty miles, only in the opposite direction. So, if you really wanted to eat at Spear's Barbecue in Linville Falls, but your riding buddies voted your choice down and you ate at Famous Louise's, you can ask for a recount! Same for Linville Caverns—if you missed it the first time, you've got a second chance.

Near the end of the ride, US 221 becomes four-lane again. At the intersection of US 221 and NC 226, the Little Switzerland Loop ride ends. If you have the energy and the inclination, turn right and follow that route backwards. Okay, ride forward, but follow the route in the opposite direction from the way it is presented here.

This adventure ends where it began, in Marion at the intersection of US 221 and US 70. Turn right for a scenic ride back to I-40 by way of the town of Old Fort. The Little Switzerland Loop ride begins at this intersection, so you might want to flip a few pages and get your butt ready for more saddle time.

RIDE ALTERNATIVES

This ride includes a little jaunt to the Blowing Rock through the town of the same name. It's not really an alternative, it's more like an option.

In Boone, you might decide to start a different ride. This route passes through the intersection of US 221/NC 105 at mile 54.2. That particular intersection is the beginning of several other rides, so take this book with you in case you decide to add some riding to your day.

At mile 71.2, you can make a left off the route onto a twisty section of US 221 and ride two miles to the entrance of Grandfather Mountain.

ROAD CONDITIONS

The roads on this ride are well banked, well marked, and have clean asphalt. The exceptions to this are near mile 7 of the ride, where US 221 is under construction. Also, there are a few rough spots on the Blue Ridge Parkway. There are several smaller viaducts near the Lynn Cove Viaduct; some of them have hard bumps where the concrete of the viaduct meets the asphalt of the Parkway.

POINTS OF INTEREST

Linville Caverns, Famous Louise's Rock House Restaurant, Lynn Cove Viaduct, Price Lake, the haunted Cone Manor House, Blowing Rock, Tweetsie Amusement Park, Boone, views of Grandfather Mountain.

Riding high, above the Blue Ridge.

RESTAURANTS

There are many places to choose from on this ride. Unless you are a very hearty eater, you'll need to take this ride many times to dine in all the restaurants along the way.

The first one you'll come to is also a point of interest for the ride. **Famous Louise's Rock House Restaurant** at mile 21 in the town of Linville Falls sits where three counties come together. The dining room has signs marking the lines for Avery, McDowell, and Burke Counties. There's one table marked as the "Liar's Table." According to the staff at Famous Louise's, there's a group of locals who sit here to share tall tales over hot coffee. Visitors to this table are required to avoid telling the truth. Menu items range from $2 for an egg breakfast to $12 for a mountain trout dinner. Lunch includes hamburgers for around $5. Whatever your taste, Famous Louise's has something for you.

Across from Famous Louise's is **Spear's Barbecue.** This place offers lunch and dinner with an impressive wine and beer list. Spear's is famous for its ribs. At $18 for a full rack of ribs with all the trimmings, you won't go away hungry. Open seven days a week from April through October, and on Friday and Saturdays November through March, Spear's fills up quickly for dinner, so make reservations early by calling 828-765-0026.

In Blowing Rock, try the fare at the **Cheeseburger In Paradise Restaurant.** This hip place has comfortable outdoor seating and tasty (but expensive) burgers. Open for lunch and dinner, this is a popular place with a complete beer selection.

Also in Blowing Rock, there are many coffee shops. It's a good break from the road and you can spend a few minutes drinking your coffee, wandering through town, and letting your hair out from under your helmet.

Boone is home to most of the national fast food chains. Local dining establishments offer Italian, seafood, steak, Chinese, and nearly everything in between. A word of warning, though—your dollars buy less here than in other parts of the country. Because the town caters to the resort crowd, plan to spend about 25% more to dine out. Stop at the Visitor Information Center at mile 53.5 to investigate all your choices for dining out in Boone.

DETAILED DIRECTIONS

MILE 0—The route begins by heading north on US 221 from the intersection with US 70 in Marion. *US 221 gets a little technical after its intersection with NC 226, due to some construction. At mile 17.8, stop in for a cool 52-degree tour of Linville Caverns. It costs $5. You'll be in the town of Linville Falls at mile 21, home of Famous Louise's Rock House Restaurant and Spear's Barbecue.*

MILE 21.7—Turn right onto the access road to the Blue Ridge Parkway. Once at the Parkway, turn left northbound. *The road toward Linville Falls (the waterfall) is at mile 22.9. At mile 27.3 there's a great overlook of Grandfather Mountain. The Lynn Cove Viaduct and information center is at mile 35.5. For a good view of the viaduct, look over your right shoulder at mile 36.6. The Blowing Rock ride begins by turning right off the Parkway at mile 45.7. The haunted Cone Manor House and Craft Center is at mile 46.3 at the end of a long driveway to the right.*

MILE 48.5—Turn left off the Parkway onto the access road to US 321 north, then turn right at the end of the access ramp to head toward Boone. *The Tweetsie Amusement Park and Railroad is on the left at mile 51. In downtown Boone at mile 53.5 is the Boone Visitor Information Center.*

MILE 54.2—Turn left onto NC 105. *Many other rides in this book begin here. Around mile 61 there's a great view of the profile of Grandfather Mountain. You'll pass through Tynecastle at mile 67.2. At mile 69.2 you'll be able to see the mile-high swinging bridge on Grandfather Mountain. At mile 71.2, the ride continues straight, but to visit Grandfather Mountain, turn left here onto US 221 north. The entrance road is two very twisty miles up the mountain. Continuing straight, you'll ride along a not-so-famous county road that cuts through an area of vacation homes and even a golf course.*

MILE 72.8—Turn left when the road "T's" into US 221. *There's a nice mountain lake at mile 74 on the right side of the road. You'll pass under the Blue Ridge Parkway at mile 82.3. The town of Linville Falls with Famous Louise's Rock House Restaurant and Spear's Barbecue are at mile 83. The driveway to Linville Caverns is at mile 86.2. Around mile 93.3 you'll suffer through a little construction traffic. US 221 intersects with NC 226 at mile 97.3. US 221 becomes a four-lane road.*

MILE 104—The ride ends where it began at the intersection of US 221 and US 70 in Marion. *Turn right here to head to the start of the Little Switzerland Loop ride (p. 106) or to cut through the town of Old Fort to get back to I-40.*

Grandfather Loop

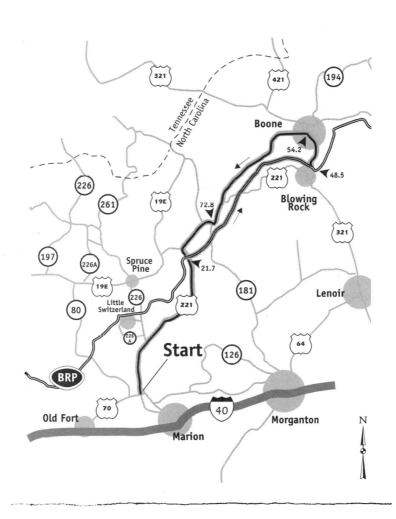

Tennessee
North Carolina

Boone

Blowing Rock

Spruce Pine

Little Switzerland

Lenoir

Start

Old Fort

Marion

Morganton

BRP

321 · 421 · 194 · 221 · 321 · 226 · 261 · 19E · 197 · 226A · 19E · 80 · 226 · 221 · 181 · 126 · 64 · 70 · 40 · 226A

54.2 · 48.5 · 72.8 · 21.7

N

🛡 **75** Interstate Highway	⭕ **28** NC State Highway	▬ Route
🛡 **27** US Highway	◇ **91** TN, VA, SC State Highway	— Other Road
	5▶ Milepost	▬▬ Blue Ridge Parkway

Blowing Rock

Blowing Rock is a quaint little town that caters to the wealthy vacationers who own homes and condos there. But you don't have to be rolling in the dough to enjoy the many cool things the town has to offer. With several great restaurants, stores, coffee shops, and the Blowing Rock itself, this town's unique setting and population make it well worth the side trip.

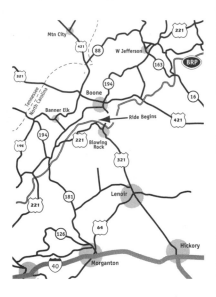

GETTING TO THE START

You'll start this ride by turning off the Blue Ridge Parkway onto US 221 near Blowing Rock. Zero your trip meter as you turn off the Parkway.

RIDE OVERVIEW

"I'll have a side order of Blowing Rock to go, please!" Admittedly short, this route is meant to be an addition to any ride you're taking on the Blue Ridge Parkway that passes near Blowing Rock. The Grandfather Loop ride passes by, but if you're touring the entire length of the Parkway, or just kicking around and find yourself near Blowing Rock, there are some things you ought to know about the place.

The town of Blowing Rock gets its name from an actual blowing rock that has an unusually strong updraft. The wind rushes up from the Johns River Gorge 3,000 ft. below. It is said that the snow "falls up" here. According to Indian legend, the Blowing Rock was the scene of a lover's leap that was thwarted by the Great Spirit who created an updraft so strong that it blew the suicidal brave back into the arms of his lover. And the wind still blows.

The town is full of unique shops and sights. You'll notice tall red poles attached to the fire hydrants to help the firefighters find the hydrants in heavy snow. That should tell you something about the annual snowfall in Blowing Rock. In fact, there's so much snow, Blowing Rock is one of the most popular ski resort destinations east of the Mississippi.

Ready to eat? Blowing Rock has everything from wine rooms and coffee shops and cheeseburger joints and diners. Yep, something for every taste. There's free parking along Main St. in the heart of downtown, so you might want to take advantage of this and explore Blowing Rock on foot.

Farther down Main Street, the ride meets US 321 and turns right to get to the Blowing Rock itself. You'll find ample signs for this private park. It costs just $4 for adults and $1 for kids to enter. (They are considering raising the rate to $5 to offset the cost of some new trails.) You'll save a dollar if you're in a group of 15 or more, but please phone ahead if you are expecting the group rate. You can call them at 828-295-7111 to confirm the price of admission and/or to get the group rate. In the park, you'll find breathtaking views of Hawksbill Mountain, Grandfather Mountain, Mt. Mitchell, and the deep Johns River Gorge. There are two gift shops and one snack bar. Most impressive is the

observation platform that seems to float above the Gorge below. Seeing the Blowing Rock is well worth $4, and if they do raise the rate to $5, it'll be worth that, too!

The ride ends at the Blowing Rock. To return the way you came, take US 321 north from the Blowing Rock and either turn left back onto Main St. or continue straight, bypassing the downtown area. Either way, you'll arrive back on the Blue Ridge Parkway in a matter of minutes. Or, you can continue on US 321 north all the way into Boone. It's up to you.

RIDE ALTERNATIVES

Instead of returning to the Blue Ridge Parkway by riding back on the same section of US 221 you rode in on, take

Rocking chairs invite you to sit a spell and enjoy the view at Moses Cone Manor on the Blue Ridge Parkway, just outside Blowing Rock.

US 221 north out of the city and back onto the Parkway, or stay on US 221 north and ride all the way into Boone.

ROAD CONDITIONS

US 221 and US 321 through Blowing Rock are well maintained, but very busy. Don't expect to ride through town quickly.

POINTS OF INTEREST

The village of Blowing Rock, the Municipal Park in Blowing Rock, the Blowing Rock itself.

RESTAURANTS

Blowing Rock is full of great places to eat. One of the most popular is **Cheeseburger in Paradise** at the intersection of US 221 and Main St. This great burger joint offers tasty cheeseburgers and sudsy beers for lunch and dinner. You'll be able to sit outside and enjoy watching the people walk, drive, and ride past. Be prepared to spend about $12 for a burger and beer combination.

The local favorite is on Main Street about a block after you turn off US 221, where you'll find **Sonny's Grill** on the left. Established in 1954, Sonny's has been serving up breakfast and lunch at reasonable prices ever since. You can plan on $2 for an egg breakfast and $5 for a lunchtime sandwich item. For a meal with some pep, try the Tex-Mex cuisine of **Tijuana Fats**. Also on Main Street, Tijuana Fats offers great food and a fun atmosphere, and is open seven days a week for lunch and dinner.

There are many places to eat in Blowing Rock. Just park your bike and blaze your own dining trail—parking is free on Main St.

DETAILED DIRECTIONS

MILE 0—Turn off the Blue Ridge Parkway toward US 221 north near Blowing Rock (there are signs directing you). *At the end of the access ramp to US 221, turn left onto northbound US 221.*

MILE 1.7—Turn right onto Main St. *There's free parking on both sides of the road.*

MILE 2.9—Turn right onto US 321 south.

MILE 3.7—The ride ends where you can turn right to reach the Blowing Rock. *You can choose to ride back north on US 321 to Main St. and to US 221 north, or follow the US 321 bypass north to avoid the Main St. area. Either way, you'll be returned to the Blue Ridge Parkway, where you can decide what to do with the rest of your day.*

Blowing Rock

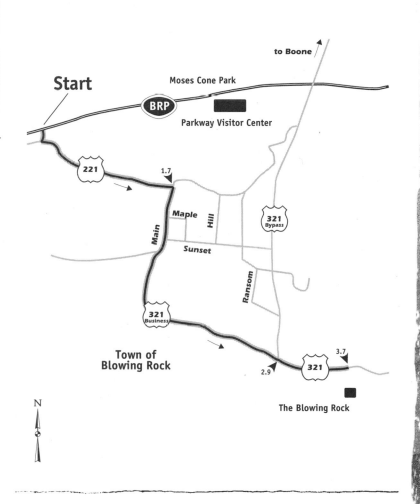

to Boone

Start

Moses Cone Park

BRP

Parkway Visitor Center

221

1.7

Maple

Hill

321
Bypass

Main

Sunset

Ransom

321
Business

**Town of
Blowing Rock**

3.7

2.9

321

The Blowing Rock

N

75 Interstate Highway	28 NC State Highway	▬▬ Route
27 US Highway	91 TN, VA, SC State Highway	▬▬ Other Road
	5 ▶ Milepost	▬▬ Blue Ridge Parkway

Watauga Loop

This route gets its name from Watauga Lake in Tennessee and Watauga County in North Carolina. It takes you from Spruce Pine, NC through Hampton, TN along the shore of Watauga Lake, and through Mountain City, TN, ending in Boone. Along the way, you'll pass an abandoned Hollywood movie set, cruise through the scenic Toe River Valley, and dine on the shore of a mountain lake. Meanwhile, the road beneath you twists like a snake. With so much to see and do on this long ride, consider making it a two-day tour.

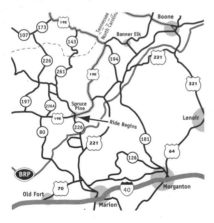

GAS

Gas is plentiful throughout this long ride. You'll find gas for sale at miles 1.6, 1.9, 4.3, 10.6, 10.8, 23.5, 25.2, 25.7, 30.1, 30.6, 40.6, 43, 55.4, 62.2, 66.2, 71.2, 71.8, 82.1, 83.9, 86.6, 91.1, 94.7, and at the ride's end in Boone.

GETTING TO THE START

This ride starts in Spruce Pine at the intersection of US 19E and NC 226. To get there from Asheville, take US 19 north from the city and then follow the signs for US 19E north into Spruce Pine. An even more scenic way to reach the starting point is to follow NC 226 from US 221. You can pick up US 221 in Marion and follow it north to NC 226, then turn left on NC 226 for a twisty ride over the Eastern Continental Divide on the way to Spruce Pine. Regardless of how you get there, zero your trip meter as you turn north on US 19E at the intersection with NC 226.

RIDE OVERVIEW

Begin by heading north on US 19E. For those of us who are curious about such things, the "E" in 19E does not mean that the road travels east. However, US 19 splits near Burnsville, NC where US 19W turns north toward Tennessee and 19E continues straight into Spruce Pine before turning north. So, for the record, US 19E is east of US 19W which is west of US 19E. *Voila!*—the mystery of E and W explained.

From Spruce Pine, US 19E is a four-lane highway for a few miles as it heads into the mountains that create the natural border between Tennessee and North Carolina. About two miles into the ride, US 19E loses the extra two lanes and becomes a friendly two-lane ribbon of asphalt. As you ride out of Spruce Pine, you're sure to notice the Flick Video on the left side of the road with the tail of an airplane sticking from its roof. One can only guess that the pilot didn't want to pay the late movie return fee!

Soon you'll be riding beside the Toe River. This river flows rich with trout and other fish sought by fly-fishers who come from far and wide to test their skills against their elusive prey. The Toe River Lodge in Plumtree caters to the hardy characters willing to stand in the current of the Toe, casting flies. You'll cross a bridge and enter the little burg of Plumtree, where you'll find the Plumtree Church on the right and an abandoned movie set on the left.

Back in 1990, Plumtree was home to the filming of the movie *Winter People*. This movie starred Kurt Russell and Kelly McGillis. *Winter People* was a romantic story in which Russell's character moved from the big city to a small mountain town and fell in love with McGillis. The story revolves around the couple falling in love in the midst of a family feud. You can visit the old clocktower that was in the center of town in the movie. The stone tower is actually made of a type of fiberglass. The bricks of the smokehouse next to the road are made of the same Hollywood set production material.

Long before the visit from Hollywood, C.W. Wilson's General Store and a log cabin stood here. First opened in 1886, the general store was also home to the post office and a dentist's office. The store closed, but relived part of its glory for the 1990 filming of *Winter People*. After the filming ended, the building began to fall into disrepair. In 1998 the roof fell in and the building that once

TOTAL DISTANCE
96.8 miles

TIME FRAME
Without stopping at any of the cool things along the way, this ride will take you just 4 or 5 hours. If you plan to do most of the activities on the route, plan a day or two (you can stay on Lake Watauga or in Mountain City).

stood two stories high is now being picked away by people scavenging the rare wormy wood from which it was built. The cabin has fared much better. You can see it next to the Toe River, across the street from the church. Look closely to see the "portholes" on the windows. These portholes were used to defend the cabin's residents from the Indians who lived nearby and occasionally attempted a raid on the place.

Leaving Plumtree, US 19E follows the narrow Toe River Valley through towns like Minneapolis and Cranberry. Iron ore mined in Cranberry was used by the Conferacy during the Civil War.

Turn left at a "T" intersection to remain on US 19E. You'll ride out of the valley, toward the town of Elk Park, and eventually to the Tennessee state line, where the King of the Road Steak House awaits. Chances are you'll smell the steaks grilling before you see the restaurant. This is a remote spot for such a good steakhouse. You'll also find a restaurant with a view a few miles farther into the ride.

About a half a mile after entering Tennessee, the Appalachian Trail crosses the highway. Watch your speed; the hikers have a long way to go to reach the end of the trail in

Maine and running over a hiker would ruin *your* day, too.

You'll ride through the town of Roan Mountain. The mountain will be on your left as you cruise through the valley. There's plenty of gas in town. To reach the top of Roan Mountain or to visit the state park of the same name, turn left onto TN 143 at mile 30.6. After leaving the town, the road becomes a four-lane highway.

You'll ride on this four-lane highway section for only a couple of miles as you near Hampton. In Hampton, turn right off US 19E onto US 321 and TN 67. You'll be leaving the busy, four-lane section behind and will be greeted with the gently sweeping curves of a great two-lane road. TN 67 and US 321 trace the south shore of Watauga Lake.

Along the shoreline are several roadside parks that are part of the Cherokee National Forest. It costs just $2 to enjoy all of these parks, and the money you spend on the parking pass is used to keep them open for future motorcycle visitors. For dining with a view, picnic in one of these roadside parks. Or, visit the Watauga Lakeshore Resort, home to a marina, motel, lounge, and restaurant. From the restaurant, the views from the dining room are nearly as appealing as the seafood that's served there. And there is more than seafood on the menu; steak and chicken dishes are also available. You'll also find fishing, pontoon, and speedboats for rent. The prices range from $8 to $40 an hour, with considerable discounts for all-day rentals. For a room or a cottage, rates start at $60 and go up to $125. It's best to call ahead to make reservations. For more information, call 423-725-2201 or visit them on the web at www.lakeshore-resort.com. The road takes a bend away from Watauga Lake, approaching a bridge

which crosses the lake. US 321 turns to the right, but the ride continues straight onto TN 67. You'll cross the Butler Memorial Bridge, soaring high above the water. The flat water below is a stark contrast to the rolling crests of the surrounding mountains. The ride passes through several small towns in the Doe Valley. The Doe Mountains are on the right side of the road and the Iron Mountains are on the left. One can only speculate how the Doe Mountains got their name, but the Iron Mountains were so rich with iron ore that the name came naturally. The road seems to flow almost straight as you near Mountain City.

Mountain City is a quiet little Tennessee town that gets its name from—you guessed it—the surrounding by mountains. The ride makes a right onto US 421, which heads south through the town in a four-lane highway with a 40-mph speed zone. Be sure to watch your speed; others are. Another route that passes through Mountain City is The Backbone ride (p. 156). You might want to take part or all of The Backbone ride while you're here, so keep this book handy as you explore the area. You'll find many thriving businesses in Mountain City. If you are in the market to replace your trusty steed, the folks at Mountain City Motorcycles will be glad to have the business. They offer Suzuki motorcycles, service, and parts.

Next to the motorcycle shop is Bizzie's. This small drive-in puts a little local flavor into fast food. Speaking of fast food, Mountain City has that, too. Just about anything you would care to order from a freckle-faced kid is available in this town. If you prefer a little more for your dining dollar, try Cook's Cafeteria. At Cook's you can look at the food before you order it so you'll know exactly what you're getting. Leaving Mountain City, US 421 snakes its way through the Stone Mountains and back into North Carolina. Along the way, it loses a couple of lanes and becomes the two-lane road we motorcyclists prefer.

Just over the Tennessee state line you'll find the King of the Road Steakhouse.

Back in North Carolina, US 421 gives you passing lanes as the traffic around you struggles to climb the steep hills. On one of the downhill sides of these hills you'll find Boone Action Honda. If the Suzuki dealership in Mountain City didn't show you something that was to your liking, try sitting on a few bikes at Boone Action Honda.

You'll begin to mix with heavy traffic as you near the outskirts of Boone. This small town has grown into a huge attraction. With winter skiing and summer sight-seeing, there are almost always tourists here, mixing with the students of Appalachian State University. Unfortunately, the U.S. dollar has been greatly devalued relative to the "Boone Dollar." A shopping spree in Boone can be much more expensive than one at a lower elevation.

US 421 becomes known as King Street as you enter Boone. Despite the previous warnings about spending money in Boone, it's worth taking time to browse the Mast General Store and many other shops that make up the shopping district along King Street. You'll find coffee shops, bagel bistros, and a couple of soda fountains.

The ride turns right onto US 221 and ends at the intersection of US 221/321/421 and NC 105. Many other rides (like the Fresco Tour) start, end, or cut through that intersection. Keep this book with you in case you want to add to your adventures.

RIDE ALTERNATIVES

At mile 52.8, you can turn to the right off TN 67 onto US 321 south and head to Boone, cutting off about 25 miles from the ride. In doing so, you'll miss the Doe River Valley and Mountain City.

ROAD CONDITIONS

All of the roads in this adventure are clean, well-banked, two-lane asphalt. Many of them have passing lanes that help make short work of the other traffic you might encounter in the mountain passes. The roads are well maintained, but expect an occasional piece of gravel in the road.

POINTS OF INTEREST

The filming location of *Winter People*; Watauga Lake with picnic areas, lodging, boat rentals, and restaurant; Doe River Valley; Mountain City, TN; Boone, NC.

RESTAURANTS

On the North Carolina/Tennessee border on US 19E at mile 26.1, try the **King of the Road Steakhouse**. Open for lunch and dinner, the house specialty is steak (about $9 for a filet). Another option is the **Lakeshore Resort** on the shore of Watauga Lake at mile 48.4. Open for dinner only (except Sunday when they open at 11 am.), seafood and ribs take center stage on the menu, and there are great views of the lake from every table. Expect to spend $10-18 for a dinner entrée.

Not as scenic but a much better dining value, **Cook's Cafeteria** in Mountain City at mile 72.7 is open from 6 am to 8 pm, offering breakfast, lunch, and dinner with prices ranging from $2 for biscuits and gravy to $8 for a roast beef dinner.

There are many **fast food** establishments along the way. One of the coolest is **Bizzie's Drive-in** at mile 71.6 in Mountain City, a classic hometown drive-in.

In Boone there are plenty of places to choose from. Beyond fast food, most are expensive. Somewhere along the way into Boone, you cross an invisible boundary. Once on the Boone side, the U.S. dollar seems to be worth only about 75 cents. This applies to hotels, too.

DETAILED DIRECTIONS

MILE 0—Start the ride in Spruce Pine, by heading north on US 19E from its intersection with NC 226. *You'll cross the Toe River at mile 12. The Toe River Lodge is on one side of the bridge; on the other is the town of Plumtree, where the movie* Winter People *was filmed. Next you'll enter the town of Minneapolis (not Minnesota, but what a great shortcut that would be). The site of the Cranberry Iron Ore mines is at mile 22.7.*

MILE 23.5—Turn left at the "T" intersection to remain on US 19E. *Enter Tennessee at mile 26.1. The King of the Road Steakhouse is on the state line. Watch for hikers at mile 26.8 where the Appalachian Trail crosses US 19E. US 19E becomes a four-lane divided highway at mile 39.5.*

MILE 42.8—Turn right onto TN 67 (also marked as US 321 south). *The town of Hampton has fuel and food. At mile 46.1 is the first of many pullouts along Watauga Lake. It costs $2 for a parking pass, which you can use at the other National Forest facilities over the next few miles. The Lake Shore Resort is on the left at mile 48.4, where you can eat dinner, enjoy the bar, rent a boat, spend the night in a cabin, or settle into a motel room. The C.R. "Doodle" White overlook (free) is on the left at mile 50.7. At mile 52.8, continue straight as US 321 turns right (turn right to begin the ride alternative.). You'll enter Mountain City at mile 70.3.*

MILE 71.2—Turn right onto US 421 south. *Bizzie's Drive-in is on the left next to the Mountain City Motorcycle dealership at mile 71.6. The Mountain Empire Motel and Cook's Cafeteria are on the left at mile 72.7. The speed limit in Mountain City is 40 mph. At mile 75.3, US 421 becomes two-lane. The North Carolina state line is at mile 82.5. If your Honda needs parts (or you need a new bike), stop in at Boone Action Cycles at mile 87.5. Enter the Boone business district at mile 94.7.*

MILE 96.1—Turn right onto US 221 south.

MILE 96.8—The ride ends at the intersection of US 221, US 321, and NC 105. *Many rides start at this intersection, so bring this book with you in case you want to do more riding.*

Watauga Loop

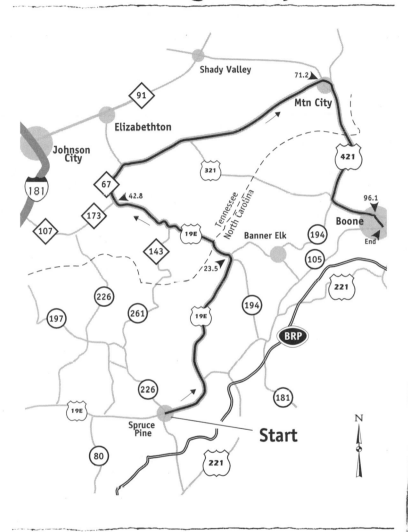

Shady Valley

91

71.2

Mtn City

Elizabethton

421

Johnson
City

321

181

67

96.1

42.8

173

19E

Boone

107

Banner Elk

End

143

194

23.5

Tennessee
North Carolina

105

226

194

221

197

261

19E

80

226

BRP

221

19E

181

Start

Spruce
Pine

221

N

75 Interstate Highway	28 NC State Highway	▬ Route
27 US Highway	91 TN, VA, SC State Highway	Other Road
	5 ▶ Milepost	Blue Ridge Parkway

GETTING TO THE START

This ride starts in downtown Boone. Getting to Boone is scenic regardless of where you start. From Asheville, take I-40 east to Marion and then pick up US 221 northbound to Boone. From the north, follow US 421 or 321 (depending on where you're starting from). Both of these roads find their way to Boone. Once in Boone itself, zero your trip meter as you head north on US 221 from its intersection with US 321 and NC 105.

RIDE OVERVIEW

What is a fresco, anyway? Sounds like some kind of lemon-lime beverage. Actually, a fresco is a painting made by applying watercolor paints to wet plaster. This ride gets its name from the interior of a church along the way, decorated with three beautiful frescoes. Now that we have that tough question answered, let's ride.

Leave the busy downtown section of Boone on US 221 north from the intersection of US 221/321/NC 105. The route makes a right turn onto US 221/421. You'll find the Boone Victory Motorcycle Dealership on the left just after the right turn. This little shop sells new Victory bikes as well as trade-ins of other models. They will service just about anything the mechanic feels comfortable with.

After passing the Victory Dealership, the ride begins in earnest by turning away from the city and onto NC 194. You'll discover NC 194 to be a quiet, two-lane road that is excellently paved and banked. Along

*T*his route will take you through tight turns, along the banks of the world's second-oldest river, and down narrow country lanes, finishing with curvy NC 88. So curvy, in fact, traffic engineers gave it the curviest number they could: 88. Lightly motored roads, lots of twisties, beautiful scenery, and the lovely paintings at the Church of the Frescoes near Baldwin make this ride long on scenery and short on traffic.

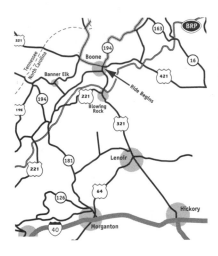

GAS
There's gas at the ride's beginning and along the way at miles 1.3, 2.9, 23.5, 24.9, 25.1, 27.1, 27.5, 30.7, 35.3, 38.3, 38.9, 48.8, 53.8, 55.6, 58.3, 62.6, and in Boone at mile 66.3.

the way, you'll ride through rolling farmland full of grazing cattle and the occasional Christmas tree farm. You won't reach any high altitudes, but there's plenty of breathtaking scenery to enjoy. There are lots of tight twists and turns, too.

You'll pass through the thriving metropolis of Todd, NC. Actually, Todd is not really a metropolis, but an old town that had its heyday in the early 1900s when the train made a whistle-stop there. Farther ahead is the left turn onto Baldwin Rd., which runs from the town of Baldwin to West Jefferson. The divided four-lane US 221 parallels Baldwin Rd. Because of this, most drivers prefer the speed and relative straightness of US 221 over the narrow twists and turns of Baldwin Rd. Motorcyclists generally prefer the road less traveled, and besides, you'll miss the Church of the Frescoes if you take the faster and more efficient US 221 to West Jefferson.

The ride to the Church of the Frescoes is a fun one. The actual name of the church is St. Mary's Episcopal, but it is better known as the Church

TOTAL DISTANCE
68.5 miles

TIME FRAME
2 hours. That includes a few minutes to view the frescoes, but does not include time to enjoy a 25-cent cup of coffee along the way. Add a few minutes to this ride if you'd like to do that.

of the Frescoes. If you can separate your butt from your seat for a few minutes, take in the sights of the Church of the Frescoes. Whether you are religious or not, you're sure to appreciate the skill and talent it took for Ben Long to create these masterpieces. Painted between 1974 and 1986, the frescoes include *Mary Great with Child*, *John the Baptist*, and *Mystery of Faith*. This church holds regular Sunday services, so time your visit accordingly.

Baldwin Rd. "T's" into NC 194 in the town of West Jefferson. The ride turns left as NC 194 takes you through the heart of West Jefferson. As you

The Church of the Frescoes sits on a grassy knoll at the edge of the town of West Jefferson.

The High Country **147**

Downtown West Jefferson boasts some not-quite-frescos, with a more local flair, on the sides of several town buildings.

ride through downtown, you'll see the Ashe County Visitor Center. Ashe County? But we're nowhere near Asheville, right? Correct—Asheville is in Buncombe County. Makes perfect sense. At any rate, West Jefferson is home to many small shops and gas stations along Main St. In just three miles, you'll be headed out of town, greeted by a wildly curvy road.

NC 88 meets NC 194 and the two roads share the pavement as you ride between Potty and Phoenix Mountains. You'll continue straight on NC 88 after NC 194 turns right. At this point, NC 88 follows the twisty banks of the North Fork of the New River, thought to be the second-oldest river on earth. You'll enjoy the curves and turns as you contemplate the age of this ancient body of water. What's unusual about this section is that NC 88 climbs and descends very little. There are no tall mountain peaks or deep gorges to ride through. There's plenty of nice scenery, though, including a spillway waterfall. Because of heavy shade over the road and its proximity to the river, this ride is cool even on the hottest of summer dog days.

There are several general stores along NC 88. They cater mostly to the local farmers and other residents. Inside these establishments, you'll discover everything from a deli serving sandwiches to a tack shop offering leather gear for horseback riding. Think of these as little "everything" shops. At one of them, (the one at mile 48.8) you'll find the 25¢ cup of coffee, so rare it has long been rumored to be extinct. Sit a spell on the log out at the gas pumps and try to count the cars that pass and don't stop in. Chances are the number will be close to zero. It seems that selling a little of everything—plus a 25¢ cup of coffee—is good for business. Now, if we could just get Starbucks to subscribe to that business model...

You'll begin a short climb out of the New River Valley and enter Tennessee. The road name changes from NC 88 to TN 67. Soon, TN 67 "T's" into US 421, where the route makes a left turn.

Unlike NC 88 and TN 67, US 421 is a busy stretch of roadway. However, it is not without its charms. You'll enjoy the passing lanes as you forge through traffic uphill. You'll reenter North Carolina, where the road name remains US 421. You'll see Rich Mountain on the left side of the road and the Stone Mountains off in the distance to the right. Also on the right side of US 421 is Boone Action Honda at mile 59.2. This dealership will be glad to sell you a new motorcycle or ATV, or service your Honda.

You'll find the road gets a little busier as you near the town of Boone. In Boone, US 421 is known as King St. There are several neat places to eat in downtown, catering to the ski crowds in the winter and the college kids in the spring and fall. One of the most nostalgic is the Boone Drug Store (near mile 67). In this modern drugstore you'll find an old-fashioned soda fountain, offering root beer floats and sandwiches, reminiscent of the place your mom used to take you when you were just a tot.

The Mast General Store has an outlet on King St. This is not to be confused with the Mast General Store of Valle Crucis. The Mast General Store in Valle Crucis opened in 1883 and the one in Boone opened as the Old Boone Mercantile in 1913. There's a soda parlor here, too, and the feel of the old general store hasn't been lost.

The ride makes a right back onto US 221 and ends where it began in the heart of Boone. A number of rides in this book use Boone as a terminus, so you might want to consider taking this book with you to add another adventure to your day.

RIDE ALTERNATIVES

At mile 19.6, the ride makes a left onto Baldwin Rd. Baldwin Rd. is a narrow two-lane road that leads you past the Church of the Frescoes. If you have no interest in the frescoes, pass Baldwin Rd., turn left onto US 221, and follow it into West Jefferson. This little detour will shave about ten minutes off your riding day.

ROAD CONDITIONS

Two-lane, clean, smooth asphalt abounds on this adventure. Unfortunately, many of the tightest turns are unmarked, so be prepared for some unexpected turns. There's very little traffic along the way, but you will encounter farm vehicles and cars going to and from the many farms along the route. Show respect for the locals and pave a good road for the motorcyclists who will follow you.

POINTS OF INTEREST

Many farms, the Church of the Frescoes, several country general stores, the New River (second-oldest in the world).

RESTAURANTS

There are many places to eat in Boone. **Fast food** is available in Boone and in West Jefferson. Along NC 88 you'll find that many of the **general stores** also offer deli food. Grab a sandwich from one of these places and eat outside next to the New River.

DETAILED DIRECTIONS

MILE 0—Head north on US 221 from the intersection of US 221/321/421 and NC 105 in Boone *(this is the intersection with the two-story Wendy's).*

MILE 0.7—Turn right at the "T" intersection to remain on US 221 north. *You'll find a Victory motorcycle dealership on the left side of the road just after this turn. They sell other bikes, too (mostly sportbikes that were traded in for new Victory cruisers).*

MILE 1.3—Turn left onto NC 194. *You'll first be thrilled to be leaving the busy-ness of Boone behind, and second, you'll be glad to find the smooth, clean, and shaded asphalt of NC 194. There's a gas station at mile 2.9 and a church made of stone at mile 19.2.*

MILE 19.6—Make a left onto Baldwin Rd. *If you find yourself at a large "T" intersection, you've gone just 50 ft. too far. Baldwin Rd. is the last left before NC 194's intersection with US 221. After turning onto Baldwin Rd., you'll see a gas station at mile 22.9 and then the Church of the Frescoes at mile 23.3. Established in 1892, this small church has been enhanced by the artwork of Ben Long since the 1970s. There's more gas at mile 23.5.*

MILE 23.9—The road ends in a "T" intersection at NC 194. Turn left. *At mile 24, the town of West Jefferson greets you with a ride down Main St.. You might want to stop in at the Ashe County Visitor Center at mile 25.4 in downtown West Jefferson.*

MILE 30.8—Go straight onto NC 88 when NC 194 makes a 90-degree right turn. *The New River is forced over a spillway at 33.5. This spillway contributes a little electricity to the area. There's a gas/deli combination at mile 35.3. Get the sandwich to go and*

dine on the banks of the New River or the North Fork River. There are many gas stations along the way. One of the busiest gas station/general stores is at mile 48.8. This is where you'll find the rare 25¢ cup of coffee, once believed to be extinct.

MILE 51.8—You'll enter Tennessee, where NC 88 becomes TN 67.

MILE 53.4—TN 67 ends at US 421; turn left. *You'll reenter North Carolina at mile 54.2. Boone Action Cycles (Honda Dealership) is on the right at mile 59.2. They are open Tuesday through Friday 9 am to 5 pm and Saturday 9 am to 2 pm. You can get a head start on the Banner Elk Loop ride by turning right onto NC 194 at mile 61.7. You'll enter Boone at mile 66. Look for the Mast General Store on the left.*

MILE 67.7—Turn right onto US 221 southbound.

MILE 68.5—The ride ends where it began at the intersection of US 221/ 321/421 and NC 105. *Many rides start and end here, so take this book with you in case you get a hankerin' for more riding.*

Fresco Tour

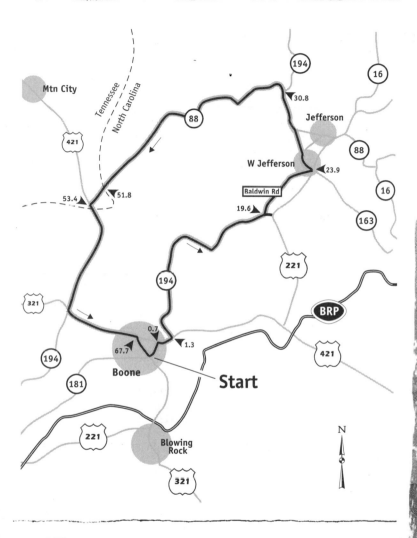

Mtn City

Tennessee / North Carolina

421

88

194

30.8

Jefferson

16

W Jefferson

88

23.9

16

Baldwin Rd

19.6

163

53.4

51.8

221

194

BRP

321

194

0.7

1.3

421

67.7

Boone

181

Start

221

Blowing Rock

321

N

Symbol	Description		Symbol	Description		Symbol	Description
75	Interstate Highway		28	NC State Highway		▬	Route
27	US Highway		91	TN, VA, SC State Highway		▬	Other Road
			5 ▶	Milepost		▬	Blue Ridge Parkway

Stations Loop

This ride takes in part of the Blue Ridge Parkway, passes the unique, motorcycle-friendly Stations Inn, rolls along the "lumpy" section of US 221, and crosses the second-oldest river in the world. Although it can be a challenge to reach the route itself, with all the great sights and fun roads it offers, it's well worth the trip!

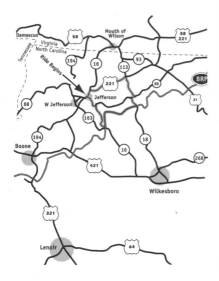

GAS

There is gas available at the start of the ride, at miles 3.8 and 41.5, and at the ride's end at mile 44.7.

GETTING TO THE START

This ride begins just east of Jefferson, NC at the intersection of US 221 and NC 88/16. You can reach this intersection by following US 221 north from Marion (that's exit 85 off I-40).

RIDE OVERVIEW

This ride starts along a quiet section of NC 16/88 through rolling hills. You'll make a right to continue south on NC 16. NC 16 continues to roll through the countryside by climbing and descending hills while making sweeping curves. Soon, you'll reach the Blue Ridge Parkway.

The Blue Ridge Parkway is well known for its great views, graceful curves, and superb surface conditions. Take advantage of the many scenic overlooks you'll pass. At the Northwest Trading Post (northwest North Carolina) you'll find a replica of an old general store. Inside is lots of cool stuff from rock candy to dulcimers, and local arts and crafts. When you're done shopping, stop in the information center to learn more about the area. The restrooms are behind the trading post.

You'll leave the Parkway by turning onto NC 18 northbound. After making the turn, you'll probably be blinded by the sun reflecting off the chrome of the dozens of bikes parked at the Stations Inn. This establishment has been catering to motorists and motorcyclists since the 1950s and has gone through some changes over the years. One important change is that they no longer pump gas. The sign at the old Esso Gas Station reads, "We pump no gas....just take you back to the past." The restaurant, general store, and motel are filled with nostalgic photos and knickknacks. While Harleys dominate the parking lot, motorcyclists of all kinds are welcome at the Stations Inn. The lines between biker, motorcyclist, touring rider, and sportbiker blur quickly in the bar.

NC 18 rolls northward through some farmland and then makes a left turn onto NC 113, which will lead you all the way into Virginia, if you let it. However, this ride makes another left turn onto US 221 at a flashing yellow light.

This section of US 221, which passes several farms on its way to the New River, is relatively straight, but don't assume you can crack that throttle wide open. For some reason, this section of US 221 was paved with "waves" in the asphalt. At the right speed, the waves are an entertaining reminder of the dime store horsy you begged your dad to give you a quarter to ride. Too fast, and the waves turn your bike from the dime store horsy into a mechanical bull dead set on throwing you! Keep your speed below 40 mph and you'll actually enjoy the ride to the New River.

The New River is second only to the Nile River in age. Before there were dinosaurs, the New River flowed to the sea. Today, you can float down the New River by paying a visit (and some cash) to the New River Outfitters in the general store next to the river. The general store is much like it was in the early 1900s, with jars of hard candy and plenty of friendly country folk to help you decide what to buy.

The New River Outfitters offer canoeing and tubing expeditions down the New River, including the shuttle

TOTAL DISTANCE
44.7 miles

TIME FRAME
Plan to spend an hour or so riding and much more time to stop in at the Stations Inn (it's a *motel*, so you might decide to stay). Add a few hours if you plan to float the New River.

back to your bike at the end of the day. Options range from a one-hour canoe trip ($11 per person) to a six-plus hour trip ($21 per person). Tubing starts at $7 for a one- to two-hour trip and $11 for a three- to five-hour trip. Reservations are highly recommended. Call 800-982-9190, find them on the web at www.canoethenew.com, or write New River Outfitters, P.O. Box 433, Jefferson, NC 28640.

The ride makes a left where US 221 "T's" into NC 16. In just over a mile, US 221 and NC 16 meet NC 88 at another "T" intersection. The ride ends there. US 221 continues south to the right and NC 16/88 turns to the left. To head toward Jefferson, Boone, Blowing Rock, Linville Falls, and Marion, follow US 221 south.

For more riding, check out the Fresco Tour ride that passes through West Jefferson, or the Mt. Rogers Scenic Byway ride that ends where this ride ends.

RIDE ALTERNATIVES

You can add about 50 miles to this ride by not turning onto US 221 at mile 31.6. In doing so, you'll miss the opportunity to take a whitewater trip down the New River. At mile 31.6 continue straight on NC 113 and into

Virginia, where NC 113 becomes VA 93. When VA 93 meets US 58, turn left, ride through the microscopically small town of Mouth of Wilson and then left onto VA 16. You'll return to North Carolina where VA 16 becomes NC 16. Follow NC 16 to the ride's end at the intersection of NC 16/88 and US 221 just east of Jefferson.

ROAD CONDITIONS

You'll enjoy the road conditions on this ride. One exception is the first 4.5 miles of US 221 off NC 113, which is best described as "lumpy." The road was paved with dips; watch your speed here to keep from being thrown from your trusty steed.

POINTS OF INTEREST

Blue Ridge Parkway, Northwest Trading Post, Stations Inn (and bar), New River Outfitters and General Store.

RESTAURANTS

The **Stations Inn** (at mile 24) opened in the 1950s, catering to the motorists who toured the Parkway. Today, it caters to passing motorcyclists and motorists, offering great food, music, a general store, and motel rooms. The rooms of the inn are decorated with the signs from old gas stations. You might check into the Esso Room or the Standard Oil Room—hence the name of the establishment.

The restaurant is decorated with biker gear, old signs, and faded photos of days gone by. The menu is unusual, too; it reads like a mechanic's price list. Instead of appetizers, you'll see "Jumper Cables & Starter Fluids." Instead of Entrees, you'll find "Total Overhaul." The beer list is titled "Fluids & Oils." Expect to spend about $8 for a sandwich and beer. If you're riding with friends, try the handmade pizzas! For lodging reservations, call ahead at

877-528-7356 or check them out on the web at www.stationsinn.com.

DETAILED DIRECTIONS

MILE 0—The start of the ride is at the intersection of NC 88/16 and US 221. *Head down NC 16/88 away from Jefferson, N.C.*

MILE 3.2—Turn right onto NC 16 after crossing the south fork of the New River.

MILE 10.2—Turn right onto the Blue Ridge Parkway access ramp and then make a left at the top of the ramp, northbound on the Parkway. *The Northwest Trading Post and Information Center (restrooms, too) is on the left at mile 12.8.*

MILE 23.7—Turn left off the Parkway onto the access ramp to NC 18, then turn right onto NC 18 at the end of the ramp. *At mile 24, you'll find the Stations Inn. Parking is on both sides of the road. The restaurant is on the right side of the road.*

MILE 26.7—Turn left onto NC 113.

MILE 31.6—Turn left onto US 221. The ride alternative begins here. *This section of US 221 is the lumpy stretch described under* Road Conditions; *watch your speed. You'll cross the second-oldest river in the world at mile 35.6, with New River Outfitters and General Store on the far side of the river at mile 35.8.*

MILE 43.4—Turn left to remain on US 221 south. *US 221 joins NC 16 for the next several miles.*

MILE 44.7—The ride ends where it began at the intersection of NC 16/88 and US 221. *Turn right to remain on US 221 to Marion and I-40, passing through Jefferson, Boone, Blowing Rock, and Linville Falls. Turn left to head back to the Blue Ridge Parkway.*

Stations Loop

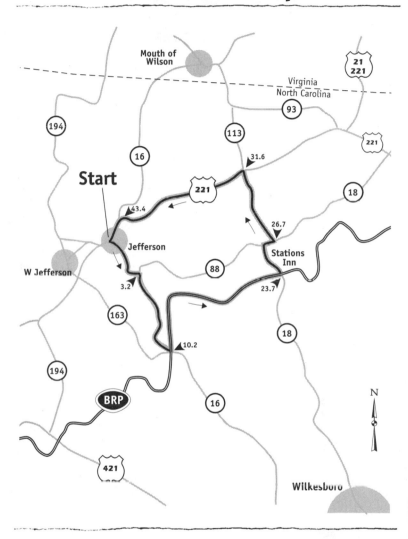

The Backbone

*T*his ride derives its name from the unusual geological formation through which this adventure will take you. Following two-lane roads that alternate between quiet stretches and wild hairpin turns, this ride has something for every type of motorcyclist. Along the way, you'll pass through several small towns and ride through an old covered bridge. Another feature most bikers will like about this ride is the nearly complete absence of other traffic. You're sure to enjoy this introduction to the great scenic byways of eastern Tennessee and southern Virginia.

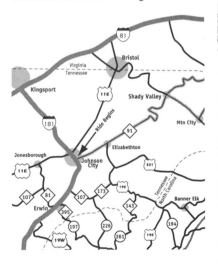

GAS

Gas is available at the start in Johnson City and Elizabethton as well as at miles 0.9, 4.7, 6.9, 11, 11.7, 12.5, 14.7, 18.2, 31.6, 44.9, 54.8, 59.3, 59.7, and 70.7.

GETTING TO THE START

This ride starts on TN 91 northbound from I-181 in Johnson City, TN. To get to that intersection from Tennessee, follow I-81 to exit 57 and southbound I-181, and follow that to exit 32 and TN 91 in Johnson City. Once at the bottom of the ramp, turn left (north) on TN 91 (*caution, TN 91 is divided here, so you'll need to cross the northbound lanes and then turn left onto the southbound lanes*). From Asheville, NC, follow US 23 north and into Tennessee. US 23 becomes I-181; take exit 32 and turn right onto northbound TN 91. Zero your trip meter as you turn onto TN 91 from I-181.

RIDE OVERVIEW

The Backbone ride starts deeper into Tennessee than any other ride in this book. As the crow flies, Johnson City is only about 15 miles from North Carolina, but since the mountains of the Cherokee National Forest make up the border between the two states, the distance by road is much longer. Heck, you won't even go into North Carolina on this ride, you'll just get really close. However, if you want to get to the many great motorcycle routes in western North Carolina, this ride will draw you to them.

You'll find that TN 91 is a busy little road. With businesses on both sides and lots of traffic, you may wonder why you're on it. After the first couple of miles, TN 91 becomes a nice, sweeping, two-lane byway as you head toward Elizabethton.

In Elizabethton, TN 91 meets US 321. The route makes a left here and takes you through another small business district. You'll see the smokestacks of the old town mill on the left side of the road as you negotiate through some traffic and weave through the fast food choices. US 321 curves left and you'll continue straight onto Elk Ave.

Elk Ave. will take you into the downtown area that was booming before they built US 321. The old buildings and businesses of the downtown area have not lost any of their charm, but they *have* lost most of their customers, who prefer to remain on the more efficient US 321 that bypasses the downtown area. As soon as Elk Ave. merges into E. Elk Ave., you'll see a tall monument in the middle of the road about five blocks in front of you. That monument is a Veteran's Memorial. As you near the monument, the ride makes a right turn onto East River St. and then left through the covered bridge.

TOTAL DISTANCE
70.7 miles

TIME FRAME
2 ½ hours from start to finish. Plan an extra hour to climb Backbone Rock or several extra hours to take advantage of the Virginia Creeper Trail.

The covered bridge was originally built in 1882 at a cost of $3000 for the structure and $300 for the approaches. Since then, the bridge has been refurbished and most of the wood has been replaced, but none of the bridge's allure was lost. Inside it, the planks that make up the driving surface run parallel with the traffic, so be careful not to let your front tire "track" into one of the grooves between the planks. On the far side of the approximately 75-ft, bridge is a small park. You can dismount there and spend a few minutes admiring the external structure.

Beyond the bridge, take the first left, which puts the Veteran's Memorial in front of you again. You'll see the courthouse past the Memorial and the county jail on your right.

It's your only chance to cross a covered bridge in any of the rides in this book, so make the detour in Elizabethton.

Nothing like making the trip from court to jail a short one, eh? The ride makes a right turn back onto E. Elk Ave. which quickly "T's" into US 321/19E.

Turn left onto US 321/19E and continue straight onto US 19E at the next traffic light. US 321 turns left and goes back into Elizabethton. From US 19E north, the ride takes the first exit to the right, back onto TN 91.

Unlike the stretch of TN 91 out of Johnson City, you won't find too many businesses along this section. A few gas stations, sure, but little else. The Elizabethton Airport will be on your left. There are a few large, privately owned aircraft hangared there; you might see one take off. The road cuts just a couple hundred yards from the end of the runway.

The Tennessee Department of Transportation (or "T-Dot," as it is known locally) has decided to widen the first few miles of TN 91 from Elizabethton. The work will take several more years to complete, so expect to see some construction until 2003. After 2003, you'll find a widened and less twisty TN 91. There are still plenty of curves ahead, so don't go thinking that because you're taking this ride in 2005, you've missed the best part.

Around mile 20 or so, the ride on TN 91 becomes wildly twisty. You'll enter the Cherokee National Forest and leave civilization behind. Under a thick canopy of trees, you'll make your way through tight turns on fresh, clean asphalt. There's little traffic on this section, so enjoy!

You'll reenter civilization by riding into the town of Shady Valley. Shady Valley is exactly that. Bounded by Iron Mountain to the east and Holston Mountain to the west, this narrow valley is surrounded by rolling

In the mood for cranberries? This tower is full of them—just kidding.

mountain ridges. The valley is home to many quiet farms. TN 91 intersects with US 421 and TN 133. At this intersection, you'll find two gas stations. These are also grocery stores, video stores, delis, and gathering places for the people who live in this quiet little valley. Shady Valley hosts a Cranberry Festival annually, but one of the locals says that cranberries haven't been grown in the valley for years. Continue straight from TN 91 onto TN 133.

TN 133 seems to mirror TN 91, leaving Shady Valley by way of several well-paved twists and turns through the Cherokee National Forest. Again, sparse traffic and superb road conditions make this ride a great one. TN 133 is paved where the old steam trains that helped get the lumber from these mountains once had their tracks. The trains would follow Beaver Dam Creek into Virginia, taking advantage of the creek's water to fill the steam boilers should they run low. Just south of Virginia, the train companies ran into a big problem; really, they ran into a wall.

Backbone Rock stands about 80 ft. tall, 20 ft. wide, and nearly half a mile long. This unusual geological feature created an enormous stumbling block for the train. The train company considered going around the rock, but that would put the train over the creek, so they decided to tunnel through it. Less than 20 ft. in length, this tunnel is known locally as the shortest tunnel in the world. Today, the train tracks are gone and TN 133 cuts through the hole created to allow the train to pass. When you near the hole in the rock, look for the extra little section they had to cut out of the top of the tunnel to allow for the train's crane to pass through. If you want to climb to the top of the rock, you may park on the road to the right of the tunnel entrance or in the parking lot to the left. The parking lot costs just $2. The money goes to the Forest Service and helps keep the place up.

If you decide to climb to the top of the rock, you're in for a heart-pounding hike. It's short, but it's vigorous. From the parking area, the trail climbs in a series of zigzags to the flat, narrow top. There are no handrails on the top, so if you have a fear of falling or a fear of heights, admire this rock from the ground. On top, you'll find a couple of wooden bridges that were built back in the mid 1980s. Spending just $200,000, a team of prison inmates refurbished this trail, built the wooden walkways, made a picnic area and developed a campground. Talk about repaying your debt to society!

After passing through the rock, you'll see the campground on the left and Virginia round the corner. In Virginia, TN 133 becomes VA 133.

On the Virginia side, the ride takes you through the town of Damascus. VA 133 "T's" into US 58 in downtown Damascus. If you're curious, Damascus used to be named Mock's Mill but its name was changed by General Imboden of the Confederate Army because he thought the town resembled Damascus, Syria (two rivers and a mountain full of iron nearby). You'll turn right to remain on the ride. The Appalachian Trail crosses through downtown Damascus, as does the Virginia Creeper Trail. You've probably heard of the Appalachian Trail, famous for stretching from Georgia to Maine, but what's this creeper all about? The Virginia Creeper Trail gets its name from the old steam trains that used to creep through the woods between Abingdon, through Damascus, and on

The shortest tunnel in the world is at Backbone Rock.

to White Top. The 34 miles of rail were abandoned not so long ago and were converted to a hiking and bicycle path. The most popular section of the trail is the 17-mile section between White Top and Damascus. It's popular because of the scenery and many old bridges it uses to cross a creek, but probably most popular because it's virtually all downhill from White Top to Damascus. Several outfitters in Damascus will rent you a bike, load you into a van, and shuttle you up to White Top. From White Top you'll enjoy a leisurely 17-mile ride through the woods back to Damascus where you'll return the bike and grab a bite to eat.

If you want to eat or stay at the Damascus Old Mill Restaurant, Inn & Conference Center, turn left at the intersection of VA 133 and US 58. Then, make a right at the Dollar General Store onto E. Imboden St. The Old Mill can be found down that road. It closed about 60 years ago and remained vacant until the spring of 2001 when some developers decided to turn the structure into a viable business. Offering fine dining overlooking Laurel Creek and first-class accommodations over the restaurant, the Old Mill is sure to be in business for years to come.

Back on the ride, US 58 makes a sharp right turn and passes a couple of gas stations. The road then turns back to the left. You'll spot the Virginia Creeper Trail on the right side of the road. On the left is the In the Country Bakery & Eatery. This little business packs a powerful punch for its size, encompassing a sandwich shop, an ice cream parlor, and even an antique shop. Open seven days a week from 6 am to 8 pm, this business really caters to bikers. By bikers, I mean bicyclists, although they'll happily serve you, too. Still, they are geared (no pun intended) mainly toward the bicyclists using the Virginia Creeper Trail.

You'll cross the Virginia Creeper Trail when you bear right off US 58 onto VA 91. VA 91 quickly becomes TN 91 as you cross back into Tennessee. TN 91 follows the banks of Laurel Creek as you ride toward Mountain City. You might want to eat the sandwich you got in Damascus at one of the many gravel pullouts on Laurel Creek.

Leaving Laurel Creek in your wake, TN 91 enters Mountain City. In downtown, turn right onto Main St. You'll find the Main Street Cafe on your right. If you didn't eat in Damascus (or if you have an appetite like mine) stop here and eat again! You can enjoy breakfast served any time and lunch and dinner served at appropriate times, seated at one of the sidewalk tables just feet from your bike. Unless you're very imaginative it won't remind you of a French cafe, but it's got pretty good food and low prices.

Main St. meets US 421 and this is where you'll turn right to cross Iron Mountain and return to Shady Valley. US 421 has a few pieces of gravel strewn out in the curves, but its asphalt is twisty and fresh, making it a pleasure to ride on.

The ride ends in Shady Valley. From the ride's end, you can continue north on US 421 into Bristol (lots of curves for the first few miles), turn right onto TN 133 and ride through Backbone Rock again and into Damascus, or turn left and head south on TN 91 toward Elizabethton.

RIDE ALTERNATIVES

If you're headed to the start of the ride from North Carolina, consider starting the ride in Elizabethton instead of Johnson City. You can do this by taking the Murder Mountain ride or the Watauga Loop to where they intersect with US 19E. Follow US 19E north into Elizabethton where you'll find TN 91 north on the right after passing the county jail on the left. To get to the covered bridge, turn left at the county jail and you'll find the bridge about two blocks down on the left.

ROAD CONDITIONS

This adventure starts with large, busy city roadways that gradually become quiet two-lane country byways. Between Johnson City and Elizabethton, TN 91 and US 321 are commercial and not what you would call scenic. US 321 is five lanes wide (four traffic lanes plus a turning lane) and relatively flat. Leaving Elizabethton, TN 91 worms its way through some construction and finally becomes the two-lane, well-banked stretch of road you have been looking for. Most of the roads are free of debris. The exception to this is the stretch of US 421 between Mountain City and Shady Valley that has gravel strewn in the curves.

POINTS OF INTEREST

The covered bridge in Elizabethton, the Elizabethton Airport, Shady Valley, Cherokee National Forest, Backbone Rock, Virginia Creeper Trail.

RESTAURANTS

Elizabethton is home to nearly every kind of **fast food** you would want to eat. In the town of Shady Valley, the **gas stations** are also home to delis.
   In the Country Bakery & Eatery in

Damascus, VA invites you to sample ice cream, coffee, sandwiches and breakfast items. Open from 6:30 am to 8 pm, seven days a week, it's sure to offer something on the menu to please you for less than $5. Also in Damascus is the **Damascus Old Mill Restaurant, Inn & Conference Center**. This beautiful structure can be found by turning left at the end of VA 133 and then turning right on E. Imboden St. (one block down). The Old Mill sat vacant on the banks of Laurel Creek for nearly 60 years, but in the spring of 2001, it was reopened offering delicious steaks, beautiful scenery, deluxe accommodations, and meeting rooms for conferencing. They don't accept reservations for dinner, which is offered Wednesday through Saturday from 5 pm to 9 pm and on Sundays from 11 am to 4 pm. The menu is dominated by their delicious steaks, but you'll also find seafood, pasta, and other dishes priced from $9 to $19. There's a good wine and beer list as well. Upstairs, the old grain rooms have been converted to hotel rooms. You will need to make a reservation for a room by calling 540-475-5121. Their rates are seasonal, so call ahead for that information.
   Mountain City, TN is also home to many fast food outlets, but for home cooking, try the **Main Street Cafe** (on Main St.) It's open seven days a week from 6:30 am to 9 pm, offering breakfast anytime for $2 to $5. Lunch is a bit more expensive with a burger and fries running you just $4. A dinner of pasta or fish will start around $9 with the menu items going as high as $17. There's also outdoor, cafe-style sidewalk seating, so your bike doesn't have to be alone while you're eating.

DETAILED DIRECTIONS

MILE 0—Turn north on TN 91 in Johnson City, TN.

MILE 4.7—Make a left onto US 321 in Elizabethton. *There's plenty of fast food and gas stations here.*

MILE 7.7—Continue straight onto Elk Ave. where US 321 curves to the left. *Elk Ave. merges into E. Elk Ave. at mile 7.9. You'll see the Veteran's Memorial sitting in the middle of the road a few blocks in front of you.*

MILE 8.5—Turn right onto East River St. (it's a right turn just before a bridge). Take your next left, and ride through the covered bridge. *Use caution here—the wooden planks that make up the riding surface run parallel to the road, creating a hazard if your front wheel finds the groove.* On the far side of the bridge, turn left and then make a right back onto E. Elk Ave. at the Veteran's Memorial.

MILE 8.9—Turn left onto US 19E north.

MILE 9.7—Exit to the right onto TN 91. *The Elizabethton Airport is on the left at mile 11. You'll start to ride through some sharp curves at mile 24.9 as you enter part of the Cherokee National Forest. You'll start into Shady Valley at mile 28.1.*

MILE 31.6—Go straight onto TN 133 at the intersection of TN 91 and US 421, in Shady Valley. *TN 133 cuts through Backbone Rock at mile 41.3. There's a gravel pullout on the right side of the road and a parking lot on the left. Picnic and campgrounds are just beyond the rock on the right and left, respectively. You'll enter Virginia at mile 41.8. Mile 44 is at the southern border of the town of Damascus.*

MILE 44.9—Turn right onto US 58 (this is a "T" intersection). *If you want to dine and/or stay at the Damascus Old Mill, turn left at this intersection. Turn right at the Dollar General Store, a block away, and you'll find the Mill on this road.*

MILE 45.1—Turn right to stay on US 58. *The road curves to the left at mile 45.4, and just beyond that curve is the In the Country Bakery & Eatery on the left side of the road, offering ice cream, coffee, crafts, and breakfast and lunch items. You'll see the Virginia Creeper Trail on the right side of the road; it's an abandoned train track turned bicycle trail.*

MILE 46.3—Bear right onto VA 91 and cross Laurel Creek. *You'll reenter Tennessee at mile 47.9 and enter Mountain City at mile 58.*

MILE 59.3—Turn right onto Main St. to remain on TN 91. *The Main Street Cafe is on the right at mile 59.5.*

MILE 59.7—Turn right onto US 421 north. *You can see a Veteran's Memorial Monument on the left at mile 60.1. Watch for gravel in the curves as you climb and descend Iron Mountain. You'll be back in Shady Valley at mile 67.*

MILE 70.7—The ride ends in Shady Valley at the intersection of US 421, TN 91, and TN 133. *Turn left to head back into Elizabethton, make a U-turn to head into Mountain City, turn right for Damascus, VA or continue straight on US 421 north toward Bristol.*

The Backbone

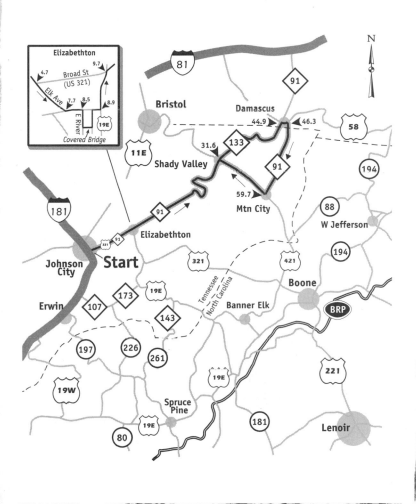

Elizabethton

Broad St (US 321)
4.7
9.7
Elk Ave
7.7 8.5
8.9
E River
19E
Covered Bridge

81

91

Bristol

Damascus

44.9 — 46.3

58

11E

31.6 — 133

194

Shady Valley

91

59.7

Mtn City

194

88

W Jefferson

181

91

Elizabethton

321

421

Boone

Johnson City

Start

Erwin

107

173

19E

BRP

143

Banner Elk

197

226

261

221

19W

19E

Spruce Pine

181

Lenoir

80

19E

Legend:

75	Interstate Highway	28	NC State Highway	▬▬	Route
27	US Highway	91	TN, VA, SC State Highway	—	Other Road
		5 ▶	Milepost	═══	Blue Ridge Parkway

Mount Rogers Scenic Byway

The shadow of the highest peak in the state, this route rolls through southern Virginia on the Mt. Rogers Scenic Byway. While never climbing Mt. Rogers's 5,729-ft. elevation, you'll have the opportunity to climb Haw Orchard Mountain (5,089 ft.) in the Grayson Highlands State Park. Along the way, pay a visit to the start of the Virginia Creeper Trail, or just settle into the road's rhythm of left, right, left, right. The real draws, though, are the superb road conditions and scenic views as you follow US 58, a smooth ribbon of freshly paved asphalt running through forests, along streams, and over mountain passes.

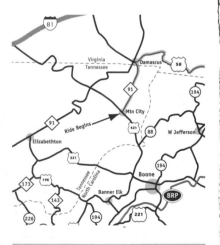

GAS

Gas is available at the start in Mountain City, at miles 5, 30.1, 42.1, 46.4, 54.4, 65.3, and at the ride's end at mile 68.

GETTING TO THE START

The ride starts on TN 418 at US 421 in Mountain City, TN. This intersection is just over a half mile south of the intersection of US 421, TN 67, and TN 91. Get to it from North Carolina by following US 421 north out of Boone. From the Tennessee side of the mountains, take I-81 to I-181 south through Johnson City, where you'll find US 431. Follow US 321 through Elizabethton and south to Hampton, then follow TN 67 along the shore of Watauga Lake, through the Doe Mountain Valley and into Mountain City. Zero your trip meter as you turn north onto TN 418 from US 421.

RIDE OVERVIEW

As soon as you turn off US 421 and onto TN 418, you'll be leaving the four-lane behind. TN 418 runs just a few blocks north where it becomes TN 91 after crossing Main St. in Mountain City. TN 91 rolls northward out of town, passing some of the prettiest and largest homes in the region. After leaving town you'll notice a creek alongside the road; that's Laurel Creek, which you'll follow through the Cherokee National Wildlife Refuge and into Virginia.

Shortly after entering Virginia, the ride makes a right turn onto US 58. As you make this turn, you'll see signs for the Virginia Creeper Trail, which used to be a train track, running 34 miles from Abingdon to White Top, VA.

The most popular section of the trail is the 17-mile stretch that runs from White Top to Damascus. Why is that section so popular? It's mostly downhill! There are several bicycle adventure services in Damascus that cater to the bicycle crowd. They rent bikes for the day, give the bicyclists a ride up to White Top, and the bicyclists finish the job by riding to Damascus. To learn more about the Virginia Creeper Trail, visit White Top Station later in the ride. For the record, no motorized vehicles are allowed on the trail.

As you begin to enjoy the rolling and undulating curves of US 58, you'll notice an old train trestle visible through the trees. This old bridge was used by the train to cross the creek, but today the bicyclists get the pleasure of speeding through the woods and over the stream. Not much creeping today, unless you're peddling uphill.

Damascus is a great stop for a bite to eat before tackling the Byway.

TOTAL DISTANCE
68 miles

TIME FRAME
2 hours is what you'll need to take this ride. Plan an extra couple of hours to visit the Grayson Highlands State Park, ride a bicycle along the Virginia Creeper Trail, or dine at Ona's Country Kitchen.

The Bear Tree Recreation Area will be on the left side of the road at mile 20.4. This recreation area offers restrooms, camping, picnic grounds, and swimming. If you're in the mood to swim, be aware that it's not a swimming pool; it's a large pond, which is just as refreshing.

You might spot some hikers as they make their way between Georgia and Maine on the Appalachian Trail. The Trail crosses US 58 at mile 25.7. If you do see some hikers, be very friendly; they probably haven't seen a stranger in a while, and no one is stranger than a passing biker!

To get to White Top Station and the "top" of the Virginia Creeper Trail, you're going to have to turn right off US 58 onto an unnamed county road at mile 29.1. There is a small sign directing you to the White Top Station. This ruggedly paved road is just a couple of miles long. The station is a replica of the old train station and was built to accommodate the many bicyclists and hikers who frequent the Virginia Creeper Trail. There's an information center inside the station and the staff loves to teach folks about the trail. The community of White Top also uses it as a community center, so don't be surprised to find some music being

If you spot one of these signs, you've found the Virginia Creeper Trail.

played there, or even a wedding going on inside.

US 58 continues rolling eastward, offering great views of the mountaintops in North Carolina to your right. There are even a few gravel pullouts along the way. For really great views, visit the Grayson Highlands State Park at mile 38.7.

The Grayson Highlands State Park will be on your left as you ride east on US 58. If you have a few minutes, or if you have all day, pay a visit to this great park. You'll start your visit by riding up VA 362 to the Park's entrance. At the entrance you'll be asked to pay $1 on weekdays and $2 on weekends to enter. You can inquire about camping ($14) at the entrance. From the entrance, VA 362 continues up Haw Orchard Mountain. About two miles into the ride, you'll come to the Sugarlands Overlook. Named for the sugar maple trees that grow on the

side of the mountain, this overlook provides great views of the Blue Ridge Mountains to the south and Kendrick Mountain to the east. Farther up the mountain there is camping, along with bridle trails used by folks who bring their horses to this area. Continuing up the mountain you'll find the parking lot for the Visitor Center. This center offers restrooms, a gift shop, and a small museum about life in the area around the late 1800s to the early 1900s. There's even an old moonshine still inside the museum, so bring your note pad! From the Visitor Center there are several trails you can take to the very top of Haw Orchard Mountain. The Twin Pinnacles Trail is one of the quickest ways to reach the craggy boulders which crown the top of the mountain. And motorcycle boots are a great alternative to hiking boots. Whatever you do, don't miss this state park.

Back on US 58, you'll ride toward Volney through a series of freshly paved and well-banked twists and turns. In Volney, the ride turns right at a gas station. Inside this gas station is Ona's Country Kitchen. Ona's offers breakfast, lunch, and dinner seven days a week.

US 58 leads you into the town of Mouth of Wilson. No, it was not named for President Wilson, rather for the mouth of Wilson Creek that empties into the second-oldest river in the world, the New River. You just had to know that, didn't you?

You'll turn off US 58 onto VA 16 southbound headed into North Carolina. As you cross the state line, VA 16 becomes NC 16. NC 16 is nearly straight, but when it isn't, it offers some nice sweeping curves. US 221 joins NC 16 southbound and the two remain together until the end of the ride near Jefferson. The ride ends where NC 16 and US 221 "T." At this intersection US 221 goes to the right, toward Jefferson, Boone, Blowing Rock, and the Blue Ridge Parkway. NC 16/88 runs to the left toward the Blue Ridge Parkway and eventually to US 421 near Wilkesboro, NC.

The end of this ride is the start of the Stations Loop ride. You might want to have this book available in your saddlebag when you finish, so you can add another adventure to your day if you wish.

RIDE ALTERNATIVES

Near the end of the ride is the town of Mouth of Wilson, VA. The ride makes a right onto VA 16 in Mouth of Wilson. You can elect to remain on US 58 for another quarter mile and return to North Carolina by way of VA 93, which becomes NC 113, leading you south to

Ona's Country Kitchen is a good place to eat and a good place to gather near the end of your ride.

NC 18 south, past the Stations Inn (biker hangout) and onto the Blue Ridge Parkway.

ROAD CONDITIONS

Clean, two-lane asphalt prevails on this ride. TN 91 from Mountain City northward runs along the banks of Laurel Creek, creating a twisty and scenic ride. US 58 in Virginia is a little patchy, but excellently banked. Despite the patches, you'll enjoy the road nearly as much as the ride itself. As you return to North Carolina by way of VA/NC 16, you'll find that it, too, is well maintained, but you'll begin to encounter more traffic. As with most rides, watch for gravel strewn into the road in the curves and be prepared for a lack of signage warning you of hazards.

POINTS OF INTEREST

The Virginia Creeper Trail, Bear Tree Recreation Area, Grayson Highlands State Park.

RESTAURANTS

Fast food is abundant in Mountain City. You might want to stop in a grocery store or sandwich shop in Mountain City and get lunch to go and eat it at the Bear Tree Recreation Area or in the Grayson Highlands State Park. If you are not the picnic type, you can give **Ona's Country Kitchen** a try. You'll find Ona's in the town of Volney, VA, at mile 46.4. Ona's is open from 7:30 am to 8 pm everyday except Saturday, when it's open until 9 pm. The menu at Ona's includes big breakfast biscuits, sandwiches and burgers for lunch, and a country dinner with all the trimmings for the evening meal. Plan to spend about $4 for breakfast, $6 for lunch and about $10 for dinner. That estimate includes the best glass of iced tea for miles around (actually, the *only* glass of iced tea for miles around, but hey, it's mighty good anyway).

DETAILED DIRECTIONS

MILE 0—Turn off US 421 onto TN 418 in Mountain City, TN.

MILE 0.5—Continue straight from TN 418 onto TN 91. *This section of TN 91 follows Laurel Creek north into Tennessee where TN 91 becomes VA 91. At mile 10, you'll enter the Cherokee National Forest. Mile 12 puts you at the Virginia state line.*

MILE 13.6—Turn right onto US 58. *Watch for bicyclists as you cross the Virginia Creeper Trail. At mile 14.5 you'll see a train trestle that the trail crosses. The Bear Tree Recreation Area is to the left at mile 20.4.*

MILE 23.3—Make a right to remain on US 58 east. *Watch for hikers as the Appalachian Trail crosses the road at mile 25.7. At mile 29.1 US 58 curves sharply to the left. To get to White Top Station, turn right here and follow that road down to the old train depot replica that is a community center and information center for the Virginia Creeper Trail. There's a gravel pullout at mile 31, offering nice views of the mountains to the south. Watch your speed around mile 36.5—there's a wild hairpin turn to the right! The entrance to the Grayson Highlands State Park is on the left at mile 38.7. Take a few minutes to ride just five miles to the Visitor Center and then a few more to hike to the Twin Pinnacles Trail.*

MILE 50.4—Turn right onto VA 16 from US 58 in Mouth of Wilson, VA. *You'll enter North Carolina at mile 54.5 where VA 16 becomes NC 16. US 221 joins forces with NC 16 at mile 67.*

MILE 68—The ride ends where US 221 "T's" into NC 16/88. *This happens to be the start of the Stations Loop Ride. If you have an hour to kill, reset your trip meter, turn to the Stations Loop ride (p. 152) and make a left. If you're done riding and are ready to start heading back to civilization, turn right to remain on US 221 south and follow that toward Boone, Blowing Rock, and the Blue Ridge Parkway.*

Mount Rogers Scenic Byway

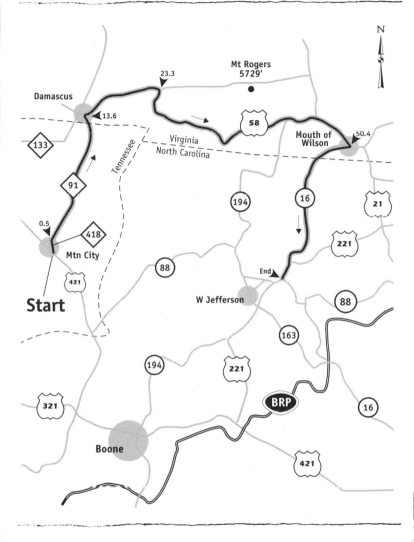

N

Mt Rogers
5729'

23.3

Damascus

13.6

58

Mouth of
Wilson

50.4

133

Virginia

North Carolina

Tennessee

91

194

16

21

0.5

418

221

Mtn City

88

Start

End

421

W Jefferson

88

163

194

221

321

16

BRP

Boone

421

75	Interstate Highway	28	NC State Highway	▬▬	Route
27	US Highway	91	TN, VA, SC State Highway	──	Other Road
		5 ▶	Milepost	══	Blue Ridge Parkway

Appendix

Places to Stay, Play, Eat, and Shop

MOTORCYCLE-ONLY RESORTS

Deals Gap Motorcycle Resort
HC 72 Box 1
Topoco, NC 28771
800-899-5550
828-498-2231
www.sporttouringusa.com
Camping, Motel, Deli, Gas, Motorcycle
Accessories, M/C Service

Blue Ridge Motorcycle Campground
59 Motorcycle Dr.
Canton, NC 28716
828-235-8350
Camping, Cabins, Restaurant, General
Store

Rider's Roost Motorcycle Resort
100 Elk Creek Rd.
Ferguson, NC 28624
336-973-8405
www.ridersroost.com
Camping, Cabins, Light M/C Service

MOTORCYCLE-FRIENDLY LODGING

Stations Inn & Restaurant
14317 Hwy. 18S
Laurel Springs, NC 28644
877-528-7356
www.stationsinn.com
Food, Drinks, Lodging, General Store

Margaritagrille Motel & Bar
P.O. Box 145
Lake Lure, NC 28746
828-625-9324
Restaurant, Bar, Motel

Dove's Rest Log Cabins
166 Dan Mar Rd.
Franklin, NC 28734
828-524-3133
dovesrest@earthlink.net
Luxury Cabins

Nantahala Village Resort
9400 Hwy. 19W
Bryson City, NC 28713
800-438-1507
www.nvnc.com
Hotel, Cottages, Restaurant

Mountain Brook Cottages
2908 Mountain Brook Rd.
Sylva, NC 28779-9659
828-586-4329
www.mountainbrook.com
Cabins, Sauna, Spa

Big Lynn Lodge
P.O. Box 459
Little Switzerland, NC 28749
828-765-4257
www.biglynnlodge.com
Hotel, Restaurant, Lounge

Fontana Village Resort
P.O. Box 68
Fontana Dam, NC 28733
800-849-2258
www.fontanavillage.com
Hotel, Cottages, Gas, Restaurant

**Switzerland Inn, Lodge,
Restaurant & Lounge**
P.O. Box 399
Little Switzerland, NC 28749
800-654-4026
www.switzerlandinn.com
Hotel, Restaurant, Lounge, on the
Blue Ridge Parkway.

Skyline Lodge & Restaurant
P.O. Box 630
Flat Mountain Rd.
Highlands, NC 28741
800-575-9546
www.skyline-lodge.com
Hotel, Fine Dining

Linville Falls Lodge & Cottages
P.O. Box 182
Linville Falls, NC 28647
800-634-4421
www.linvillefallslodge.com
Spear's Barbeque Restaurant, Motel,
Cottages

Pisgah Inn
P.O. Box 749
Waynesville, NC 28786
828-235-8228
www.pisgahinn.com
Gas, Restaurant, General Store, Hotel

Lake Lure Inn
P.O. Box 10
Lake Lure, NC 28746
828-625-2525
www.lakelureinn.com
Restaurant, Hotel

Watauga Lakeshore Resort
2340 Hwy. 321
Hampton, TN 37658
423-725-2201
www.lakeshore-resort.com
Motel, Cottages, Restaurant, Boat
Rentals

Hot Springs Spa & Campground
315 Bridge St.
Hot Springs, NC 28743-0428
800-462-0933
www.hotspringsspa.com
Camping, Cottages, General Store

Bridge Street Cafe & Inn
P.O. Box 502
Hot Springs, NC 28743
828-622-0002
www.bridgestreetcafe.com
Bed & Breakfast, Restaurant

**Damascus Old Mill Restaurant,
Inn & Conference Center**
215 West Imboden St.
Damascus, VA 24236
540-475-5421
Hotel, Conference Center, Restaurant

PARKS

National Park Service
EMERGENCIES & ACCIDENTS:
800-PARKWATCH (800-727-5928)

Blue Ridge Parkway
199 Hemphill Knob Rd.
Asheville, NC 28803
828-298-0398
www.nps.gov/blri

Great Smoky Mountains National Park
107 Park Headquarters Rd.
Gatlinburg, TN 37738
865-436-1200
www.nps.gov/grsm

Roan Mountain State Park
1015 Hwy. 143
Roan Mountain, TN 37687-3623
800-250-8620
www.tnstateparks.com
Camping, Cottages, Swimming pool,
Educational Information, Scenic
Overlooks

Caesars Head State Park
8155 Geer Hwy.
Cleveland, SC 29635
864-836-6115
www.southcarolinaparks.com
Backcountry camping, Nature Center,
General Store, Scenic Overlook

Mt. Mitchell State Park
Route 5 Box 700
Burnsville, NC 28714
828-675-4611
Restaurant, Tent Camping, Scenic
Overlooks, Gift Shop, Information

Grayson Highlands State Park (VA)
829 Grayson Highland Lane
Mouth of Wilson, VA 24363
540-579-7092
Reservations: 1-800-933-PARK
www.dcr.state.va.us
Camping, Trails, Gift Shop, General
Store, Overlooks

RESTAURANTS WHERE RESERVATIONS ARE RECOMMENDED

The Mountain House Restaurant
1801 Geer Hwy.
Cleveland, SC 29635
864-836-7330

Bridge Street Cafe & Inn
P.O. Box 502
Hot Springs, NC 28743
828-622-0002
www.bridgestreetcafe.com

Paddler's Pub
Bridge St.
Hot Springs, NC 28743
828-622-0001

The Golden Horn Restaurant
48 Biltmore Ave.
Asheville, NC 28801
828-281-4676

Barley's Taproom & Pizzeria
42 Biltmore Ave.
Asheville, NC 28801
828-255-0504

Heiwa Shokudo, Japanese
87 N. Lexington Ave.
Asheville, NC 28801
828-254-7761

MOTORCYCLE SHOPS

I've attempted to list as many local motorcycle shops here as possible, but this list should not be considered exhaustive. Also, remember that shops do occasionally change ownership and/ or product lines.

Asheville Motorsports
100 Buckeye Access Rd.
Swannanoa, NC 28778
828-686-5500

Blue Ridge Yamaha
2576 Hwy. 221N
Marion, NC 28752
828-652-9403

Boone Action Honda
8483 Hwy. 421N
Vilas NC 28692
828-297-7400

Clint's Outback Cycle Works
883 Smokey Park Hwy.
Candler, NC 28715(near Asheville)
828-665-4753

Dal-Kawa Cycle Center
312 Kanuga Rd.
Hendersonville, NC 28739
828-692-7519
www.dalkawa.com

Dragon Works
Deal's Gap Motorcycle Resort
HC 72 Box 1
Tapoco, NC 28771
800-889-5550
www.sporttouringusa.com

Easyriders
(Titan,Triumph, & Indian Motorcycles)
2925 N. Roan St.
Johnson City, TN 37601
423-928-7534

Gene Lummus Harley-Davidson, Inc.
1000 US Hwy. 70
Swannanoa, NC 28778
828-298-1683

Green Spring Sport Center, Inc.
739 Cummings St.
Abingdon, VA 24211
276-628-6237

Harper Discount Yamaha
1108 Spartanburg Hwy.
Hendersonville, NC 28792
828-692-1124

John's Garage & Motorcycle Repair
611 Swimming Pool Rd.
Hampton, TN 37658
423-725-3182

Longview Cycles
4273 Georgia Rd.
Franklin, NC 28734
800-210-8043
828-524-8043

M R Motorcycle & Marine
774 Hendersonville Rd.
Asheville, NC 28805
828-277-8600

Motorcycle Medic (Steve Thorness)
Asheville, NC
828-299-9480

Mountain City Cycle
341 S. Shady St.
Mountain City, TN 27683
423-727-8475

Myers Ducati, Husqvarna, Moto Guzzi & Triumph Motorcycles
1125 Sweeten Creek Rd.
Asheville, NC 28803
828-274-4271

Precision Cycles
4475 US Hwy. 441 South
Sylva, NC 28779
828-586-9955

Pure Sports ATV & Marine
563 Rosman Hwy.
Brevard, NC 28712
828-884-7766

**Racing Station
Harley-Davidson Accessories/
NASCAR Collectibles**
2989 Tynecastle Hwy. #2
Banner Elk, NC 28604
828-898-3500

Rodney's Cycle & Motorcycle Salvage
1109 N. Main St.
Greer, SC 29651
864-877-5449

Schroader's Honda
Intersection of US 64 & I-26
Hendersonville, NC 28792
800-445-5934
828-693-4101

Scooter Tramps
535 Tunnel Rd.
Asheville, NC 28805
828-298-6161
www.scootertramps.com

Strick's Cycle Shop
180 Patton Ave.
Asheville, NC 28801
828-252-4238

Tour Sport BMW
1431 Laurens Rd.
Greenville, SC 29607
864-232-2269

Waynesville Cycle Center
Great Smoky Mountains Expressway
W. Waynesville, NC 28786
800-648-5831
www.waynesvillecycle.com

MOTORCYCLE ADVENTURES SERIES
by Hawk Hagebak

Motorcycle Adventures in the Southern Appalachians—North Georgia, Western North Carolina, East Tennessee

Motorcycle Adventures in the Southern Appalachians—Asheville NC, The Blue Ridge Parkway, NC High Country

OFF THE BEATEN TRACK MOUNTAIN BIKE GUIDE SERIES
by Jim Parham

Vol. I: Western NC—The Smokies

Vol. II: Western NC—Pisgah

Vol. III: North Georgia

Vol. IV: East Tennessee

Vol. V: Northern Virginia

Vol. VI: West Virginia—N. Highlands

Tsali Mountain Bike Trails Map

Bull Mountain Bike Trails Map

ROAD BIKE SERIES

Road Bike Asheville, NC: Favorite Rides of the Blue Ridge Bicycle Club
by The Blue Ridge Bicycle Club

*Road Bike the Smokies:
16 Great Rides in North Carolina's Great Smoky Mountains*
by Jim Parham

*Road Bike North Georgia:
25 Great Rides in the Mountains and Valleys of North Georgia*
by Jim Parham

WHITEWATER PLAYBOATING

A Playboater's Guide to the Ocoee River
by Kelly Fischer

Playboating the Nantahala River: An Entry Level Guide
by Kelly Fischer

FAMILY ADVENTURING

Natural Adventures in the Mountains of Western North Carolina
by Mary Ellen Hammond & Jim Parham

Natural Adventures in the Mountains of North Georgia
by Mary Ellen Hammond & Jim Parham

A note to the reader:
Can't find the Milestone Press book you want at a bookseller, bike shop, or outfitter store near you? Don't despair—you can order it directly from us. Write: Milestone Press, PO Box 158, Almond, NC 28702; call us at 828-488-6601; or shop online at www.milestonepress.com.

We welcome your comments and suggestions regarding the contents of this book. Please write us at the address above or e-mail us at: masa2@milestonepress.com.